SPIRITUAL EXERCISE

tone, stretch and strengthen your faith

To Juanita,
With much love—
So good to see you again!
Helen Parker Knudop

SPIRITUAL EXERCISE

tone, stretch and strengthen your faith

Helen Krudop

Ambassador International
GREENVILLE, SOUTH CAROLINA & BELFAST, NORTHERN IRELAND

www.emeraldhouse.com

SPIRITUAL EXERCISE
tone, stretch and strengthen your faith

ISBN 978-1-932307-19-1

Cover design & page layout by David Siglin of A&E Media

Ambassador International
427 Wade Hampton Blvd.
Greenville, SC 29609, USA
www.emeraldhouse.com

Ambassador Publications
a division of
Ambassador Productions Ltd.
Providence House
Ardenlee Street
Belfast
BT6 8QJ
Northern Ireland
www.ambassador-productions.com

The colophon is a trademark of Ambassador

This book is published in association with
Patti M. Hummel, President & Agent
The Benchmark Group LLC, Nashville, TN
benchmarkgroup1@aol.com

Dedication

To the glory of God

Workout Topics

Introduction

Great! If you have opened this book, no doubt you are interested in a finding a fitness program that will help you get you in shape! If that's the case, you are invited to experience this unique exercise course designed to tone up your spiritual life, stretch your faith, and strengthen your heart toward God. As with any type of exercise, it will require a regular commitment on your part. Its value will depend on the time you are willing to invest in it. My prayer is that you will challenge yourself to new heights as your relationship with God continues to develop throughout this book.

This spiritual fitness curriculum is based on what I have learned from studying the Bible and is reinforced by personal experiences as I have walked with God. I give full credit for its creation to Jesus Christ, who inspired me to put on paper what he placed in my heart. The topics originally unfolded over a period of months for a Bible study at my local church as God led me through each phase of the workout. At the time, I was struggling with health issues, which made it impossible for me to exercise physically. Perhaps that is what makes "spiritual" exercise even more meaningful to me.

The format of this book is conducive to group study as well as individual reading enjoyment. One of the benefits of studying in a group is having the opportunity to share your own personal experiences. It's also inspiring to hear the faith-walk stories of others. Just like any exercise program, it is a lot more fun and perhaps easier to stay on task if you approach it with friends. However you choose to use this book, I pray that God will give you personal revelations and unique faith experiences of your own as you take this journey to spiritual fitness. May God bless you!

About the Author

God chose to place me in a family where Sunday school and church attendance was a common occurrence. I grew up knowing God as three distinct beings—the Father, who created all things; the Son, Jesus, who died on a cross and was gloriously resurrected; and the Holy Spirit, who is called our counselor. I knew *about* God, but I didn't really *know* God.

As a youngster I enjoyed roaming my family's farm in Nebraska. I can remember listening to the wind whistling through the trees and the wheat fields, thinking how hollow and forlorn it sounded. It seemed to match my inner thoughts as I searched for the reason for my existence. Who am I? Do I have a special purpose? What is this insatiable yearning I feel deep within? These were seldom-shared questions that came to mind in those early years.

When I moved away from home to go to a Christian-based college, I began to expand my shallow understanding of God and his universe. I experienced people of other cultures and backgrounds and listened to how God was working in their lives. It was intriguing, but still not enough to draw me in totally.

Then I married and had children. The years that followed produced an increased awareness of the sinful nature that surfaces in each of us. I must admit, I found it easier to see the flaws in others than to acknowledge my own shortcomings and weaknesses. Those were the years when our culture strongly emphasized the "look-out-for-number-one" attitude, and it seemed natural for me to get caught up in that…at least for a while. As I look back now, I see what a selfish person I was then.

But God had better plans for me, and he was working behind the scenes! He gently connected me with several Christian groups that helped me to grow in my relationship with him in a personal way. I began listening to Christian radio stations and teaching tapes, going to weekly Bible studies and reading the Bible on my own.

Then one day I raised my heart to God and accepted Jesus as my personal Savior and Lord of my life. In doing so, I received a very special sign of God's presence in my life with brilliant flaming light as he filled me with the Holy Spirit. That was definitely a turning point for me in my faith walk. I experienced true love for God and for His people. It made me so joyous! My attention was drawn to the needs of others rather than my own thoughts and desires. Several years after that God lifted a stronghold of fear from me in a prayer time. Again, another turning point! I felt a new freedom to be the person God wanted me to be.

Since that time God has continued to work in my life in amazing ways. My husband accepted a call into full-time ministry right about the time our children were marrying and starting families of their own. At the same time God called and equipped me to serve as his helpmate in ministry. God has allowed us to remain close to our children and grandchildren, and over the years I have experienced an abundance of opportunities to nurture them in the faith. Some of those stories are included in this book. In addition, my husband and I have the awesome privilege of influencing people from many different walks of life in the congregations and communities we serve. I realize the importance of staying in the Word, but I also know it's not enough just to learn. I have to share it. So...thank you for the opportunity of sharing it with you!

Chapter One

Back to the Basics –
Is Spiritual Exercising for Me?

For most of my life I have been sporadic in my approach to physical exercise. It's not the lack of desire to be healthy and physically toned that stops me. It's making myself take that first step and, more importantly, having the "stick-to-itiveness" to remain faithful to it.

There are two important elements in establishing any exercise routine. First, you must recognize the need for active participation. For any exercise to be beneficial to your health and wellbeing, your involvement is absolutely essential. Good results don't just happen without effort. Unless you work at it, the outcome is generally unsatisfactory. Secondly, it's important to have confidence that the exercise program can indeed make a difference in your life. Once we set our minds to being successful in our efforts, we generally do succeed because we have the incentive to continue through the process.

I have a medical condition that affects my muscles, so I approach exercise cautiously. I've learned (*the hard way!*) to depend on specific instructions from my physician and exercise trainer so that I don't start down the wrong path and end up doing more harm than good. I've even been given a handout with drawings that show me specifically how to approach each movement I am to do. I find it quite helpful, and when I'm first learning an exercise I rely on it heavily so that I do the right thing.

The exercise program in this book is designed to tone and shape you spiritually rather than physically. If that's what you're looking for, you are on the correct path! It will be to your benefit to make good use of a specific "handbook" in this exercise, too. In fact, you might even have it on your bookshelf already. It's the Bible! If you don't have your own personal copy yet, I encourage you to get one and keep it close at hand for reference as you exercise your spirit. There are many different styles and translations available. Select one that is easy for you to read and understand.

To begin with, you will learn some basic information that is foundational to your Christian walk. So go ahead! Ask yourself the question, "What do I have to gain from this spiritual exercise?" Then, take the challenge to exercise your way to a better understanding of God and what he has to offer you specifically. And, whatever you do, don't quit exercising!

We All Start In The Same Condition

There is one attribute we all have in common regardless of who we are. It has nothing to do with our race, gender, creed, physical ability, mental capacity or economic status. It isn't influenced by what part of the world we call home or what our experiences have been. It's a quality that may not always be apparent in some folks; nevertheless, it's there. What is the commonality? You can seek out the answer for yourself by referencing these specific verses in your Bible handbook—Romans 3:23, Isaiah 53:6 and 1 John 1:8. What do they have to say about the condition of people in general? What do they reveal about you personally?

The Bible is clear on one thing—every human being is infected with sin. No one is exempt according to Romans 3:23. None of us on our own measure up to God's requirement of perfection. We "turn astray" (Isaiah 53:6) wandering off like lost sheep rather than following the leadership and guidance of our Good Shepherd. It should be obvious to every one of us that we don't always do the right thing. However, we can become good at convincing ourselves that we're really not hurting anyone with an occasional half-truth, rude comment behind someone's back, flirtatious remark or vile thought. At times we get inflated views of ourselves, reasoning that our slate is relatively clean compared to the next person. However, we are only deceiving ourselves if we think we don't sin (1 John 1:8). We may be able to fool others or even ourselves into believing that we are not all that bad, but there is no way we can fool God. He knows the truth. He knows how we really are.

Everything Has Its Price

Life is governed by rules. We talk about rules of nature, rules of the road, rules of conduct and rules of a particular game or sport. When a rule is broken there is always a consequence, although it may not be experienced immediately. What does God think about breaking the rules? Look at the following Bible passages to determine the price for sinning—Genesis 2:16-17, Romans 5:12-14, Romans 6:23. What is the penalty for disobeying God? What does this penalty mean to you specifically?

God created a perfect world in the beginning. There was no sin. The first people on earth had everything they could possible want. But God did issue some guidelines for Adam and Eve. They could partake of anything they desired in the garden except for the tree of the knowledge of good and evil. God told them that if they did eat from it, they would surely die.

> "In actuality, death is the opposite of life."

Some people believe that death is simply a state of nonexistence— no big deal. Nothing can be further from the truth. In actuality, death is the opposite of life. Spiritual life is conscious existence in communion with God. Therefore, it stands to reason that spiritual death is a conscious and perpetual existence of being separated from God. What a terrible state to be in! That is exactly what happened to Adam and Eve when they ate of the forbidden fruit. They were separated from God. Because of their sin, they were no longer allowed to be in God's presence. Sin and death entered the world through Adam, and we all inherited that same condition. The price for sin is spiritual death—separation from God. If you look further into Adam and Eve's story in the early chapters of Genesis, you will quickly learn it is not a pleasant thing to experience.

The Ultimate Payment Has Been Made!

After sin entered the world, God instituted the law. But, no matter how hard anyone tried, no one could keep it perfectly. Therefore, God established a system for people to offer sacrifices to make up for their sins. According to Nelson's Illustrated Bible Dictionary, sacrificial offerings were "offerings to God in Old Testament times by which man hoped to atone for his sins and restore fellowship with God."[1] God's people offered the best of their lambs as an offering to God until God provided a method by which man's penalty for sin could be paid in full and fellowship with God could be restored. What is the ultimate sacrifice or payment for sin according to Hebrews 9:11-15, 24-28? And, is it necessary for you to add to this payment according to Hebrews 10:10 and verses 17-18?

In Jesus Christ's death on the cross, he became the ultimate sacrificial offering. Jesus is referred to as the "Lamb of God that takes away the sins of the world." (See John 1:29.) When Jesus went to the cross, he took our sins with him. In fact, the Bible says that he became sin for us, even though he himself did not sin (2 Corinthians 5:21 NIV). God will not allow sin to remain in his presence. Therefore, Jesus experienced separation from God in death—the required payment for sin. No wonder Jesus cried out in a loud voice, "My God, my God, why have you forsaken me?" (See Matthew 27:46.) Jesus didn't experience this separation from God because of his own sin, but because of yours and mine. There is nothing else we can contribute to the payment for sin. Jesus did it all.

What could have been God's motivation for such a selfless act displayed in his only unique Son? According to John 3:16-17 it was his overwhelming love for mankind—a love so perfect and so complete that it is beyond our human understanding. We merely accept it by faith.

The Choice Is Yours!

Everyone likes choices. No one—*especially* one who is strong-willed—wants to be told what to do! Somehow it seems less threatening if we have options.

My daughter-in-law is a well-respected teacher and a fabulous parent. Over the years I have noticed her keen effectiveness in offering choices as she deals with children. One thing in particular I have observed is that she gives only two choices, even when more options might be a possibility. I'm sure her reasoning is to make the selection process easier for the child and for herself. If multiple choices are presented, it slows down the whole decision-making process. It's much more effective to say, "It's either this...or that." That provides clarity for the child and discourages arguments and pleas for alternatives.

God offers options, too! From the very beginning of time, man was created with a "free will." We have a freedom of choice in spiritual matters. We make the decision, and there is

> "God offers options, too!"

always a consequence for our choice. God's choices come in pairs, too. We can choose life, or we can choose death. We can accept or reject his plan of salvation. There is no "middle ground" option. To the church folk in Laodicea, God put it this way, "You are neither hot nor cold. I wish you were one or the other! But since you are like lukewarm water, I will spit you out of my mouth!" (See Revelation 3:16 NLT.)

God placed the very first people on earth in a beautiful setting—a garden brimming with gorgeous greenery and luscious fruit. They were free to eat anything they wanted with the exception of the fruit of one particular tree. As long as they were obedient to God, the outcome was good. They would continue to enjoy all of the benefits placed before them in the garden. However, if they chose to eat of the tree God had specified as forbidden fruit, the result would be just the opposite—death. Two alternatives—and the choice was theirs.

Jesus is very clear on our options and the resulting consequences in Mark 16:16. In his words, "Anyone who believes and is baptized will be saved. But anyone who refuses to believe will be condemned." The gospel-writer, John, puts it this way, "All who believe in God's Son have eternal life. Those who don't obey the Son will never experience eternal life, but the wrath of God remains upon them" (John 4:36 NIV).

Each of us has been given the choice to accept the free gift of God's forgiveness and love through Jesus Christ, or we can turn our back on it. Each has the ability to choose life or death. Have you made your choice?

What's Your Response?

At this point you may be thinking, "I don't ever want to be cut off from God. I want to know that I will experience eternity in heaven. But how can I be certain? Is there something I must do?"

Yes, simply believe and receive. Salvation through Jesus is actually a gift according to Ephesians 2:8—a gift we receive by faith. That means there is nothing any of us can do to earn it. But just like any other gift, we won't reap the benefits of it unless we take it and make use of it. Jesus bought the present of eternity for each of us at the expense of his own life on the cross. We receive it by accepting and enjoying the gift in faith.

Making this choice is not something to be taken lightly; it is life changing. Choosing to accept the free gift of eternal life influences how we think, act and speak. "For

> "Making the choice...is life changing."

if you confess with your mouth that Jesus is Lord and believe in your heart that God raised him from the dead, you will be saved. For it is by believing in your heart that you are made right with God, and it is by confessing with your mouth that you are saved" (Romans 10:9-10 NLT). The choices made in our hearts and spoken out through our lips will be reinforced in our acts of obedience as we put this wonderful gift to work.

Take your Bible in hand and read Matthew 11:28-30. In these words you will find direction and clarity for your life. Do you feel weary? Are you tired of carrying a load of worries? The invitation is extended to come to Jesus, give him your heavy burdens and learn everything you can from him. He wants to lighten your load, gently teach you and give you peace and rest in your spirit. Get your heart involved. Confess with your lips that Jesus is Lord. Remember that Jesus paid the price for your sins. That payment is a gift to you, and there is nothing you can boast about achieving on your own. So simply confess your sins and renew your commitment to God regularly. If you have never made that commitment, I invite you to do so now by praying the following prayer:

Prayer of Commitment

Almighty God, I do believe Jesus Christ is your Son, the Savior of the world. I know that while Jesus was on the cross, he took all my sins upon himself and suffered the agony of separation from God in death so that I don't ever have to experience that myself. He took the punishment I deserved for my sin.

I believe that Jesus didn't stay in the grave. He was resurrected from the dead after three days and proclaimed victory over sin's power in my life. That's so awesome! Your love for me is beyond my ability to comprehend!

Jesus, I need you in my life. Without you I am nothing. I am so sorry for my sins. Come and live in my heart. Be my guide and constant companion and give me peace of mind and heart. Thank you, Jesus! Amen.

Be Confident In Your Decision—The Results Will Last Forever!

You can trust God's Word. Read and reread 1 John 1:9 every day: "If we confess our sins to him, he is faithful and just to forgive us and cleanse us from every wrong." That cleansing is like a spiritual shower. Oh, it feels so good to be clean!

Getting started in this spiritual exercise program might have been more than you bargained for. But if you truly have made the commitment to accept the free gift offered by Jesus, rest assured that you are showered up and spotlessly clean in God's sight! You can know for certain that you will live eternally in heaven. Even though your physical body will die someday, you will never have to experience the horror of spiritual death. YOU are living eternally with God, so read on!

Chapter Two

Suiting Up

Now that you've made the choice to step out in faith and accept the wonderful gift of spiritual life, are you ready to spend some time strengthening your faith through continued exercise? Good! Let's get started!

When possible I love to work out at the local fitness center. It just seems to help me keep more on target if I'm sharing the whole exercise experience with other people. It encourages me to see others that already appear to be reaping the benefits of their efforts, even though my pace may be a lot slower than some of them. They inspire me to keep on task.

There is a sign at the entrance to the work out area that says, "Participants must wear proper exercise attire. No jeans or street shoes allowed." As I look around I do notice that most people seem to be wearing similar clothing—the type that moves easily as they work out. Most definitely everyone has on athletic shoes that seem to offer great support.

Just as wearing suitable clothing is essential when you exercise physically, so it is important to "dress" properly for your spiritual walk. The Bible gives clear instruction on what to "take off" and "put on." As part of your spiritual workout for today, read the following sections from your Bible handbook to see what insight each gives about proper wearing apparel for your spiritual walk—Ephesians 4:21-24 and Colossians 3:5-15. (Now don't let this threaten you to quit exercising! Remember, it will get you going on the right track.)

I don't know about you, but I absolutely love to shop! One of my favorite pastimes is browsing through clothing stores with a friend. It's always interesting to see what is new in the fashion market. However, when I do make a purchase it often takes me a while to start wearing it. The old, familiar garments are what I reach for first thing in the morning. I feel most comfortable with them.

The scripture passages above speak distinctly about getting out of our rut of the "old and comfortable" and begin putting on some new garments. As we journey down the path of faith, we are to put on new mannerisms, striving to become more like God. We are to take off our tattered and stained clothing of the past—things like immorality, impurity, lust, evil desires, and greed. Then we are to put on fresh new garments like compassion, kindness, humility, gentleness, patience and forgiveness. Foremost, we are to be clothed in love. Through faith we become clothed in Jesus Christ himself. Isn't that amazing? What a wonderful covering that is!

> "The Holy Spirit provides the new attire; we step into it!"

Did you know that every article of spiritual clothing mentioned above is a gift to you from God? However, you still have to put them on. They won't do you a bit of good unless you are wearing them. We live in a world where sin, strife and struggles are all around, and these coverings are our protection from the elements. John Wesley, a primary figure in eighteenth century evangelical revival and founder of Methodism, taught that after we have accepted God's saving grace, we are to move on in God's sustaining grace toward perfection. The Holy Spirit provides the new attire; we step into it! We leave behind the old familiar sin-stained articles of clothing.

Now, let's take a look at clothing ourselves with the armor of God mentioned in Ephesians 6:10-18. It consists of six pieces—a belt, a breastplate, special shoes, a shield, a helmet and a sword.

That does not sound like something we normally would have in our closet! Yet, the type of armor described here is readily available to us for the asking.

Why do you suppose we need to put on armor? Verse 11 in Ephesians 6 tells us why. It's so we will be protected against the elements of the "unseen world," the crafty plans of our number one enemy. Satan and his evil forces are always busy working behind the scenes trying to get us to think the truths of the Bible are just a big farce. He would love nothing better than to lead us astray from Christianity. He wants us to think that our battles are with people, but they are not. In actuality they are with Satan himself. He is behind every one of our skirmishes.

The good news is that Satan and his army have been defeated and disarmed by Jesus! The devil may like to entice and torment, but in the end he is powerless (Colossians 2:15). As Christians, there is absolutely no need to worry about what he might do to us because we have been given authority over him (Luke 10:19).

So, if Satan has been defeated, why do we need armor? Because Satan does still rule the unbelieving world, and his presence is all around us. Although he has no direct authority over the true believer, he does have the freedom to tempt and harass Christians. Our minds are his favorite battleground. If he can trip us up in our thinking, we're just one step away from being lead astray in our actions as well.

It's easy for me to identify the areas in my life where Satan is hardest at work. Beyond a doubt, busyness tops my list. It's quite common for me to have three or four projects going at the same time. My husband would tell you that I have been this way long before multitasking was vogue! The problem is that it's so easy for me to avoid taking the time to properly restore myself physically, emotionally and spiritually. I work to the point of exhaustion, and I know that is not pleasing to God. In the very beginning of time, God taught by example the importance of setting aside specific time for rest.

Another favorite trick of the devil is to challenge my desire for perfectionism by being quick to point out every imaginable flaw in me as well as in other people. If I'm not careful, I can get drawn into being critical. That leads to negative talk, which leads to challenged relationships, which leads to resentment…and the ripple effect goes on.

What are your personal battles? It is important to identify them in your own mind so you can truly experience the benefit of putting on each piece of armor as your protection against them.

Here's exactly what we are to do when we face our battles. "Stand firm then, with the belt of truth buckled around your waist, with the breastplate of righteousness in place, and with your feet fitted with the readiness that comes from the gospel of peace. In addition to all this, take up the shield of faith, with which you can extinguish all the flaming arrows of the evil one. Take the helmet of salvation and the sword of the Spirit, which is the word of God" (Ephesians 6:14-17 NIV).

The apostle Paul was imprisoned during the writing of the book of Ephesians. From his prison cell he could have seen a Roman guard dressed in a full suit of armor and began to visualize how each piece could be used to describe a Christian's protection from evil in the spiritual realm. With that in mind, let us examine the armor in detail to best understand its application.

Belt of Truth

Long robes were typical apparel for men in Paul's day. That being the case, a soldier would have to gather up all that cloth and secure it in place with the belt (truth) so he could move more quickly in battle. For the soldier the belt had another important purpose. It held in place two other vital pieces of the armor. The breastplate (righteousness) was attached to it as well as the sheath for his sword (the Word of God). In his book, *The Invisible World*, Greg Laurie surmises that if the enemy stripped a soldier of his belt, not only would his robe fall down and trip him, but he would probably lose his sword since the breastplate was loosened and the sheath could very easily slip off.[1] The belt may not be a particularly impressive piece of the armor, but it certainly was essential.

Likewise, the belt of our spiritual armor—truth—is vitally important for our protection from our enemy, the devil. Remember all of the biblical truths we discovered in the first chapter of this book? It is essential that you keep them firmly in place in your heart and mind.

The opposite of truth is lies. Satan is often called the "Father of Lies." Deception is his business. He wants us to remain in a state of uncertainty and doubt about a lot of things, especially where our salvation is concerned, because he knows that the truth will set us free from his stronghold (John 8:32-34).

Think back to your own personal battles. What lie is the enemy trying to tell you? What really is the truth? Don't forget that the Bible is full of truths about every imaginable subject. Read it! Surround your mind with it before, during and after each and every attack of the enemy so you won't trip and fall. If you aren't sure just where to read, invest in a small Bible promise book arranged by topics of concern or ask your pastor to help you get started on the right track.

Breastplate Of Righteousness

The breastplate protected the vital organs (heart and lungs) of the soldier. If the soldier did not wear his breastplate securely, he could lose his life with just the right attempt from the enemy. That is serious business!

Likewise, the devil stalks like a lion, trying to damage the hearts of Christians. The only way it is possible is if you loosen your belt (compromise what is truth), which loosens your breastplate of righteousness.

What is righteousness? How does anyone become "in right standing" with God? Satan would like us to believe that it's our behavior that makes us right in God's sight. Then he reminds us of all our failures. Part of what he's saying is true, and that's what makes Satan's lies so effective. One of his favorite tricks is half truths—just enough truth in it to make us think that perhaps he's right. When we start hearing Satan's lies about our worth we need to remember this fact: we can't ever measure up to what is "right" on our own efforts. Paul says with sincere passion in Philippians 3:8-9 NIV, "I consider everything a loss compared to the surpassing greatness of knowing Christ Jesus my Lord, for whose sake

I have lost all things. I consider them rubbish, that I may gain Christ and be found in him, not having a righteousness of my own that comes from the law, but that which is through faith in Christ—the righteousness that comes from God and is by faith."

The only way we can be in right standing with God is by accepting the fact that Jesus stepped in to take our place for the deserved punishment—death. We don't deserve God's mercy and forgiveness, but it's by God's grace, through faith, that we receive it. Keep your breastplate on by trusting in Jesus. It will protect your heart from the enemy.

Shoes of Peace

We're marching in God's army now so how we cover our feet is very important, just as a soldier's footwear is a very essential part of his attire for firm footing. The shoes of a soldier in biblical times are often depicted as a type of sandal with straps up the leg to hold them very securely in place.[2] They may have had studs on the bottom, like golf shoes, to aid in traction when the soldier had to walk through rough terrain or climb a steep incline.

Likewise, the Christian life often can be an uphill battle. It is not unusual to encounter some opposition from family and friends who may not yet be walking with the Lord. They may view your beliefs and comments as fanatical. You may experience ridicule or rejection. Therefore, it is essential to strap on your "shoes of peace" securely.

"Dig in your heels!"

These peace-walking sandals are an absolute necessity when we find ourselves encountering those irritating stones in the path, too. If you are anything like me, you probably feel a slight elevation in blood pressure when things don't go quite like you had anticipated. Allowing that tension to fester accomplishes nothing but increased stress for everyone involved. Remaining peaceful when the going gets rough is not always easy, but it is a very effective tool against the enemy—so dig in your heels!

How can you "walk in peace" in the midst of your battles? Isaiah 26:3 tells us it is possible if we keep our thoughts focused on God.

It is only by trusting in Jesus for every aspect of our lives that we can even begin to experience the peace that is beyond all human comprehension. Remind yourself often that true peace of mind is actually a gift from God. It is a result of the Spirit of God within us. There's nothing like this kind of peace. You can choose to walk in that peace every day!

The Shield Of Faith

The soldier's shield probably was a large, heavy object made of metal. The metal served as fireproofing and protected the soldier from the flaming arrows of the enemy. Roman soldiers often linked their shields together to create a wall of protection against the dangerous attacks.[3]

In spiritual terms, Satan is going to fire his flaming arrows at you. What symbolic things could these arrows represent? Think of the things that attack you. They could be arrows of immorality, lust, hatred, envy, pride, jealousy, anger, doubt, worry, or any other kind of sin. They come in all sizes and shapes but often they are in the realm of our thoughts.

Do you ever wake up in the morning and find yourself "hit" by one of these fiery darts in your thoughts before you ever get out of bed? And then, do you go one step further, following through on those thoughts as the day progresses? If that's the case, the devil jumps right in with accusations like, "...and you call yourself a Christian, huh?"

How do you repel those darting arrows? With your shield of faith, that's how! Faith is actually a gift from God. (I'll talk more about that in chapter 3.) In order for faith to be beneficial, you must accept it and use it—just as you would any other gift. Hold up your shield and use it to repel the fiery darts of the enemy. Speak out of your mouth that you are a child of God, and that you are "saved by grace, through faith, and that not of yourself...it is a gift of God, not of works, lest any man should boast" (Ephesians 2:8,9). Most of all, don't forget to "link up" with other Christians for an even greater impact against the evil forces that attack.

The Helmet of Salvation

For years my daughter has participated in a two-day cycling adventure to raise funds for a well-known charity. She puts much time and effort into training for the event and is very aware of safety precautions in bike riding. The rule in her household is that you don't leave the premises on your bike without wearing a helmet, even if the distance traveled is going to be short. Head injuries from bicycle mishaps are a common occurrence in hospital emergency rooms and are often the result of not wearing a helmet.

The first century soldier's helmet was no different in purpose than the helmets of today—to offer protection from a blow to the head. Without it, serious injuries or even death could result.

Likewise, your spiritual helmet can save your life in the heat of a spiritual battle. It is protection for the mind—your thinking and understanding. Paul calls it the helmet of salvation with good reason. If we doubt our own personal salvation we will find ourselves helpless in fighting the enemy. The same holds true if we allow our minds to be exposed to rubbish of sin.

Did you know that sin is more than just actions and deeds? It's something within your heart and mind that leads to a wrong action. There's good reason that your mind needs to be protected. God wants to go deeper in you and change your thought patterns so that you no longer even desire in your mind the things that are sinful. He offers you salvation through the sacrificial blood of Jesus Christ, a means of protection against the very thoughts that are the beginning of our sinful actions.

> "God wants to go deeper in your mind."

Be cautious about what things you put in your mind. What are you listening to? Are the televisions shows, music and movies you listen to riddled with bad language and worldly thoughts?

We can't stop Satan from knocking at the doors to our minds, but we don't have to let him in. I like the illustration Greg Laurie describes it in his book, *The Great Compromise*. He says when someone you don't want to talk to comes to your door, what can you do? Have someone else answer the door! Likewise, the next time one of those "fiery darts" comes knocking at the door of your mind, you can ask someone else to answer. Say, "Jesus, would you mind getting that?!"[4]

The Sword Of The Spirit—The Word of God

All of the previously mentioned pieces of armor are for defensive purposes. This final piece of equipment can be used for offense as well as defense. You can attack the enemy with this one and send him running!

Many believers have all of their armor in place, but they never use their sword, the Word of God (the Bible). They leave it in the sheath. You can display your Bible in a prominent place in your home or even carry it around with you very impressively. But unless you read it, study it, contemplate its meaning for you and even take steps to commit portions of it to memory, it will not do you much good. When we fill our minds with God's Word, God brings it to our recall when the enemy strikes, enabling us to combat the lies of the enemy with God's truth. We can even be aggressive in speaking out biblical truths before the enemy tries to strike. It will render his efforts powerless. It's so important to be more than just defenders where Satan is concerned; we need to be aggressors wielding our swords!

Read Matthew 4:1-11, which is a vivid example of how Jesus used the Sword of the Spirit when confronted by the enemy. After Jesus was baptized and filled with the Spirit, he spent 40 days and nights in the wilderness fasting and praying. At the conclusion of that close time of fellowship with his Father, the devil came to him three times and tried to lure him into sin. All three times Jesus handled it the same way. What did he do? He quoted scripture! He combated the enemy with the truth.

God expects us to do the same thing. God's Word has been preserved throughout the ages as a priceless heritage for us. It's our sword! It's our sure defense when trouble comes. Satan does not like us to use this mighty weapon, and he tries everything in his power to keep us from studying it and retaining it. He tries to "snatch it away" and keep us from understanding or remembering it. [For further study, read the parable of the sower in Matthew 13.]

It's not unusual to struggle with reading, understanding and retaining the Word of God. The reason we do is because the enemy is always trying to stop us. He knows if we read it and apply it, it will render him powerless in our lives. That alone should be incentive enough for us to read it daily! We can choose to be proactive!

Why not begin by reading the book of Ephesians. It's a great book (only 6 chapters) written by the apostle Paul to one of the early churches. It explains how God adopted us into his family through his Son, Jesus. It talks about the change that takes place in us when we accept Jesus as Savior and become alive! It says that salvation and faith are gifts to us from God—ours for the accepting. It demonstrates how we can be renewed in our minds and spirits. It gives directions for living our lives as husbands and wives, as parents and children, as workers and supervisors. It illustrates the armor of God, which we've been studying, and it tells us how to pray.

"Choose to be proactive!"

Another helpful suggestion is to write particular scriptures on index or recipe cards and carry them with you. For starters, use Ephesians 2:8-9, John 3:16-17, 1 John 1:8-9.

Then add new ones each week. Read them over and over again—when you are standing in line, riding in the car, waiting for an appointment, etc. Saturate yourself with God's Word. By doing so, you are keeping your sword sharp and ready!

The word of God is living and powerful, sharper
than any two-edged sword!
Hebrews 4:12

Chapter Three

Faith-Stretching Warm Up

Now that you are familiar with some of the basic truths in your exercise handbook, and you have been properly instructed in what to wear for spiritual exercise, it's time to begin stretching those faith muscles. Remember to keep your handbook open for ready reference. Also, *do not* rush through this warm up exercise. Take the time to ponder each question and scriptural reference for optimum benefits.

Defining Faith

How would you describe faith in your own words? Look up Hebrews 11:1 and see if you need to add to your definition. Faith is not just an abstract thing according to this verse. It is something concrete that you can hold on to; it has *substance* even though you cannot see it.

It's not unusual for any of us to say we have faith in God when we see a glimmer of hope or some kind of evidence that things are going to turn out the

> "Faith leads to trust in spite of circumstances."

way we would like them to. But the real challenge of faith comes when the going gets rough and we can't see the answer we're looking for. It doesn't take faith to believe something that already exists or that we can already see. Quite the contrary is true. Faith leads us to trust in spite of circumstances.

The Quest Study Bible defines faith as "abandoning all trust in our own resources, abilities and reasoning—the things we see. It means relying instead on things we cannot see—God's promises, provisions and concern for us." It goes on to say that "an inner attitude alone does not define faith. For faith to be present, action is required. Faith proves itself by its obedience to God."[1]

Nelson's Bible Dictionary describes genuine saving faith as "a personal attachment to Christ, best thought of as a combination of two ideas—reliance on Christ and commitment to Him." Faith not only is depending on the death and resurrection of Jesus Christ as the basis for forgiveness of sins and entrance into heaven, but it is also "a personal commitment of one's life to following Christ in obedience to His commands." It describes faith as a part of the Christian life from beginning to end and goes on to say that "in modern times, faith has been weakened in meaning so that some people use it to mean self-confidence. But in the Bible, true faith is confidence in God or Christ, not in oneself."[2]

Claiming Faith

Now read the entire chapter of Hebrews 11. It is full of examples of men and women who acted in obedience to their faith— Abel, Noah, Abraham, Sarah, Isaac, Jacob, Joseph, Moses' mother, Moses, the Israelites, Joshua, and Rahab. This "Hall of Faithfulness" is a remarkable collection of social winners and losers, all of whom are now with God because of their faith.[3] If time permits, go back into the Old Testament and read the specific stories about each of these individuals. Verses 13 and 39 of the eleventh chapter of Hebrews tell us these people were commended for their faith *before* they actually received the promises for which they were hoping. That's how it should be with us as well.

Perhaps you are beginning to get a little clearer picture of what faith is all about. Now you may be asking yourself these questions.

"Do I really have faith? How can I know for certain? If I don't have faith, how could I 'get' it?"

According to Romans 12:3, God gives everyone a measure of faith. That faith is the means by which we accept the gift of salvation offered so freely to us all. This same faith set in action allows us to accomplish the tasks God has assigned each of us in order that God's work might be completed on this earth. We cannot boast about doing anything to achieve this gift of faith. It comes as a special present from God. But just like any other present we might receive, we must accept it in order to benefit from it. If we leave a gift unopened, it won't do us any good. In fact, if we do not remove the wrapping and look inside, chances are we won't even know what the gift really is. It's the same with the gift of faith. It's up to each of us to claim the measure of faith God gives us. We open that gift by hearing and studying the Word of God (Romans 10:17).

Faith In Action

Jesus repeatedly commented on the ability of faith to bring results. The New Testament is filled with fascinating stories of faith in action—people from all walks of life utilizing the gift of faith and experiencing incredible outcomes.

In the fifth chapter of Mark's gospel we find a wild man who was delivered from demonic strongholds; a well-known religious leader, whose deceased 12-year old daughter was brought back to life by the hand of Jesus; and a sickly, frail women in a crowd of people gathered around Jesus, whose believing heart prompted her to reach out and touch the hem of Jesus' garment for healing as he passed by her—faith in action.

Luke tells us about the amazing faith of a Roman officer, whose valued slave was sick and near death (Luke 7:1-10). He had utmost respect for Jesus, not feeling worthy to have Jesus make an appearance in his home. Yet, he believed that Jesus had authority over the illness his slave was experiencing. "Just say the word from where you are, and my slave will be healed," he invited. Jesus was quick to comment to the surrounding crowd that he had not seen such astounding faith in all of Israel. At that very moment the slave was completely healed—faith in action.

Look around you. What stories of faith in action do you see? What have you experienced in your own life?

A number of years ago my husband accepted God's call to become a full-time minister. Simultaneously, God called me to a full-time role as his helpmate in this new venture. It brought about a drastic change in our lifestyle. At the time we were settled into a beautiful home with an in-ground pool in a nice, suburban neighborhood. We both had good careers that provided fairly generous incomes. Taking the step into full-time ministry involved leaving our home of nearly 20 years and moving to a parsonage, which was provided by a rural church circuit where we began our first pastorate. My husband's income was drastically reduced from what we had been accustomed to, and my income was severed completely in my new role as an unpaid servant.

In the meantime, our suburban home remained on the market for sale for over half of a year. Of course, that meant continued house payments out of one meager salary. But we were so zealous about our new calling that we weren't concerned; it was easy to trust in God's provision—and God did certainly provide! Every time we look back on that period in our lives, we marvel at how we managed everything financially. The truth of the matter is, *we* didn't manage it—God did! My husband often said, "God pays for what he orders!" God had directed us into ministry, and we knew that he would take care of our needs.

> "God pays for what he orders!"

The gospel writer, Luke, records a conversation between Jesus and his disciples in chapter 17. They asked Jesus a question that is not uncommon to us, "Show us how to increase our faith." Now that's a true request for faith stretching if I've ever heard one! Jesus' response to them is mind-boggling. He tells them if they only had a speck of faith they could uproot a mulberry tree, known for its deep roots and stability. Matthew tells the same story using the example of moving a mountain. I believe Jesus is not emphasizing the size or amount of faith as much as he is putting the faith into action. What good is faith if we don't use it? Just like working a muscle in our body improves our physical strength, so putting our faith to work releases spiritual power.

Faith's Opposition—Doubt

You've just heard some pretty amazing examples of faith in action. In Jesus' own words, it only takes a small measure of faith to accomplish great things. But what about doubts? Have you experienced them? Are they normal?

Read the story of one man's struggle with doubts in Mark 9:14-24. This father desperately wanted to believe Jesus could heal his son who was controlled by an evil spirit. But his approach to Jesus was not one of surety. Rather, he said *if* you can do anything for the boy, take pity on us (vs. 22). Jesus responded, *"If I can?"* Then he went on to explain that everything is possible for those who believe (vs. 23). The father immediately exclaimed that he did believe, but he asked Jesus to help him beyond his doubts.

I think it is normal to have doubts from time to time. Don't let them frighten you. Like this father did, give your doubts to Jesus. Ask Jesus to help you overcome them, remembering that God is the source of your faith. The very one who places the faith within you will be faithful to see it grow to perfection (Hebrews 12:2).

Then Comes The Testing!

In our early years of full-time ministry, my husband, Len, and I were like newly weds who were given a huge present. We were head-over-heels in love with God, with our new parishioners and with each other. (*Although we had been married for about 30 years, Len even carried me over the threshold of the parsonage when we moved in!*) It seemed like life couldn't get any better.

But then came the testing. When the excitement settled down we began to experience situations that tried our patience as well as our faith. Friction between fellow-believers and their family members seemed to be a common occurrence. We would go through demanding and stressful times of trying to put out fires. We spent countless hours on our knees praying for marriages, differences of opinions and arguments. (*Now that I think about it, I'm not sure we always remembered to put on the armor for our own protection when we found ourselves drawn into the midst of those battles.*)

Thank God for his insight from 1 Peter 1:3-9 regarding the testing and stretching of our faith. I invite you to read and reflect on these verses as part of your faith stretching exercise for today. These words gave my husband and me the assurance that God was protecting us through the tests and trials we faced and the hope to look forward to the joy ahead. They can do the same for you.

Is your faith being put to the test? REJOICE! It is God's way of perfecting the faith that is in you. Your faith is more precious than gold. Its genuineness is tested and proved by fiery trials, just as fire is used to purify gold so that the end product is only the best. God allows our faith to be tested so that we can experience the contrast between our weaknesses and God's infinite strength.

Don't deny God the refining process in your life. It truly will be a "faith-stretching" exercise, and the results will be thrilling! So, thank God for the gift of faith that is being refined in you, and keep on *s-t-r-e-t-c-h-i-n-g!*

Chapter Four

Oh…,This Is Painful!

Anyone who has begun a physical exercise program knows the pain and soreness that can result when muscles are first stretched and toned. "No pain, no gain" is a common phrase among many training athletes.

Personally, I'm not the most disciplined person when it comes to exercising. When I do go to the fitness center after a sustained period of absence, you can believe I feel the effects on my body. If you've exercised at all, you know what I'm talking about! The muscles I use when I work out become more apparent the day after I exercise as the pain sets in. But it's a good kind of pain—it assures me that my workout was not in vain.

Similarly, you can be certain you will feel the affect as you grow and mature in your faith walk. You may have noticed that being a Christian does not exempt you from painful experiences. In fact, there are probably times when you seem to encounter more than your share of physical illness or injuries, mental anguish, emotional distress or perhaps even pain and sadness in your spirit as your faith undergoes testing.

Is God at work in the pains you encounter? He certainly is! Your handbook, the Bible, provides valuable insight for any area in which you may be experiencing distress. So, stretch out those faith muscles of yours and get ready to learn how to deal with the physical, emotional and spiritual trauma in your own life from the very best teacher—Jesus Christ!

Physical Pain

The eighth and ninth chapters of the book of Matthew contain numerous examples of people turning to Jesus with bodily afflictions. We will look specifically at five of these stories in the passages listed below. As you read each story, try to answer these two questions: In what way did each person approach Jesus for healing? How did Jesus respond in each instance?

Story #1: Matthew 8:1-3

In this passage, a man with leprosy approached Jesus in the most respectful way he could—by kneeling before him. This act, in itself, depicted the leper's attitude towards Jesus as one who was to be honored, respected and reverenced. As he addressed Jesus, he referred to him as "Lord"—one who has authority. He went on to say, "If you are willing, you can make me clean." By these very words, the leper acknowledged the power of Jesus to heal, but his statement left the choice in the hands of Jesus.

How can you follow the leper's example? Have you ever given honor to Jesus by physically kneeling before him? Do you acknowledge Jesus as Lord of your life—the one who is "in charge"—and leave the decisions regarding your life up to him?

Jesus responded to the man's request by actually *touching* him to bring about his healing. That is significant because according to Old Testament laws, lepers were ceremonially unclean, and to touch them was forbidden. *(To learn more about these laws read Leviticus 13-14).* By touching the man rather than just speaking a word of healing, Jesus demonstrated that he cared more about the leper's immediate need than adhering to rigid interpretations of rules. Instead of becoming unclean himself, Jesus brought cleansing to the leper by his touch. Think about how Jesus could touch you in your circumstances today. Is there an "unclean" area of your life that you should be inviting Jesus to touch?

Story # 2: Matthew 8:5-13

A centurion was a Roman military officer who oversight of about 100 soldiers.[1] In this story the centurion came to Jesus asking for help for his servant who was paralyzed and suffering with pain. Jesus responded, "I will come and heal him." The centurion's reaction to Jesus' comment demonstrates his unusually strong faith. Even though this man was not of Jewish decent, he understood the spiritual authority that Jesus had over sickness. He compared it to his own authority over his soldiers in that he could just speak to them to "Go," "C   d it would be done. He
                                          of authority over bodily
                                          ng faith of this Gentile
                                          rehend who he was. He
                                          ytic servant by merely

> The Word of God is
> alive and powerful!
> ~Hebrews 4:12

sus need our faith in
is "No." God has un-
elp from us. Further-
faith automatically brings healing.
many miraculous healings are definitely *linked* to faith. Jesus often performed miracles for those who already believed to help build up and strengthen their faith, and sometimes his miracles led people to faith that did not previously believe.

Story # 3: Matthew 8:14-17

Here Peter's mother-in-law is healed of a fever. In this case, no one asked Jesus for help; Jesus just saw a need and responded. Once again, the healing came as a result of a personal touch. Apparently, the healing was instantaneous, for she got up and began to serve Jesus. Do you react to Jesus' personal touch on your life with the same kind of gratitude? How easy it would have been for this woman to just go about her daily routine, forgetting the miraculous thing Jesus had just done. If we stop and think, there are probably many instances in our lives where Jesus removed a fever from us or from one of our loved ones. Have we given him proper acknowledgement? Do we serve him with grateful hearts?

Story # 4: Matthew 9:18-25

This passage contains a double-whammy! First, a local church leader came and knelt before Jesus asking him to come to his house and lay hands on his daughter who was already dead that she might live. While Jesus was on His way to the deceased girl's home, a Jewish woman who had severely hemorrhaged for 12 years pressed through the crowd to get to Jesus. This was quite risky on her part, since her chronic bleeding condition was probably from the womb, rendering her unclean and a social outcast according to Levitical law.[2] No doubt she risked her life in order to seek Jesus out in the crowd and touch the hem of his garment. "If I can just touch His clothes I will be healed," she thought (vs. 21). The only thing she had going for her was belief and hope. Notice the affectionate term Jesus calls her—daughter. Was she healed? Yes, she was! What did Jesus say was the reason for the healing? He gives credit to her faith.

And what about the girl who had already died? How did the crowd respond when Jesus said, "She's not dead but only asleep" (vs. 24)? Jesus used that terminology because death is really no different than sleeping for believers, whom Christ will raise when he returns. Do you suppose "seeing was believing" after Jesus raised her to life? I imagine the mocked laughter of the crowd turned to sheer amazement.

Story # 5: Matthew 9:1-7

In this case, Jesus' response to a severe physical handicap was one of a spiritual nature. Rather than saying, "You are healed," he said, 'Your sins are forgiven." The church folks of that day didn't understand this at all, and they accused Him of blasphemy. Jesus' response to them is fantastic! He simply says, "Which is easier to say, 'your sins are forgiven' or 'get up and walk?'" What a thought-provoking question that is. How would you respond? The miracle that followed proved that Jesus not only had the ability to heal physically, but he also had true authority to forgive sins—something these church leaders knew only God could do.

Do you believe that God, through Jesus, can and does forgiven your sins? Do you believe that God can and will bring healing to your body? Which is easier for you to believe?

Story # 6: My Story!

From little on I knew that Jesus' death and resurrection brought forgiveness of sins. Somehow that seemed fairly easy to believe. But for many years I was skeptical about physical healings, wondering if they really took place in this day and age. I never doubted that God was capable of healing today; I just wasn't sure that he still healed the sick as miraculously as he did when Jesus walked this earth.

There were certainly times when I did pray for God's intervention in my health. You know from my stories early on in this book how I tend to take on more responsibilities than I should. The thing I didn't always realize is how my abundance of energy was paying its toll on my body. Also, it was hindering others from being active in God's kingdom because I was always busy covering all the bases.

I have struggled at times with various health issues that seemed to curtail my activities, especially in my church community. There have been occasions when I could not physical play the keyboard or lead worship, as was customary. It's difficult for me to let others step in and cover things that I deem "my responsibility." But God gently and lovingly began to show me how the work in his kingdom could and would get done without my help. I watched as others stepped in to do things in many instances much better than I could have done. It was invigorating for me to see how God could draw out the talents and gifts he had placed in others. They simply needed some encouragement and an opportunity to use them.

Then one day it happened! On a summer morning after breakfast, I began to experience a distinct feeling of discomfort in my back and abdomen that started out vague and reached its crescendo in pain so severe I could not stand up. In a blur of activity I found myself being hauled off in an ambulance to a local hospital. I spent most of the following week in the hospital undergoing tests and getting my nutrition from the IV bottle that hung by my bedside. Tests revealed a condition that would require further treatment and special diet when I was finally allowed to come home. I looked as sick as I felt—I could tell by the sympathetic expressions on the faces of my family and friends.

An appeal came from my daughter, "Mom, you need to get out of the house for a little while." She invited me to go with her on a Friday evening to a women's faith-building event where my all-time favorite singer/speaker, Sheila Walsh, was to be on stage. The music and message were so refreshing and uplifting, and I knew in my heart that God was at work bringing both physical and spiritual restoration to me.

I continued on the upswing over the next several weeks. Actually, I felt better than I had in a long time, but my specialist still ordered several extensive tests to follow up on my condition. The tests revealed what I already knew in my heart. My doctor's words were, "I have no explanation for it, but I have to declare you healed!" I absolutely LOVED his choice of words! Jesus, himself, couldn't have said it better! To God be the glory!

> "I declare you healed!"

What Have We Learned About Physical Healing?

Can we expect physical healing from God today just as the people in the Bible stories did? YES! But we must remember, healing—how, when, and by what means—is God's sovereign choice. In all the miracles of healing recorded in the Bible, there is no set "formula" to guarantee healing. However, just from the few situations we have examined we can learn some things:

- ❖ Seek Jesus for who he is, not for what you can get. Kneel before him; worship him; touch him.
- ❖ Know that Jesus genuinely cares about your needs and does not want to see you suffer.
- ❖ Understand, like the centurion, that Jesus has the ability to heal by just saying the word.
- ❖ Believe, trust, and hope—and let God take care of the rest. Often God is teaching us in the process.
- ❖ When you or someone you know experiences supernatural healing, the response should be one of gratitude and service to God.
- ❖ Know that Jesus can and does have the ability to heal our spirits (*your sins are forgiven*) as well as our bodies (*take up your bed and walk*).

As Matthew states in chapter 8 verse 17, this is a fulfillment of the prophecy spoken in Isaiah 53:5 (NIV) in the Old Testament, "He was pierced for our transgressions, he was crushed for our iniquities; the punishment that brought us peace was upon him, and by his wounds we are healed."

Emotional Pain

There is another kind of pain that we all experience at different times in our lives—emotional trauma. Sometimes we refer to this kind of pain as "heartache." There can be any number of causes for emotional pain, but quite often lack of love or a feeling of rejection is the culprit. Rejection attacks everyone, and it can be profoundly painful. Examples of this type of emotional pain are divorce, abandonment, abusive treatment, or the death of a loved one. Other forms are more subtle such as feeling ignored or "left out," being the victim of rude behavior or comments, or just plain loneliness. What are some examples of emotional pain in your life?

Our children were early grade school age when we moved to a new area several states away from where they had lived the first years of their lives. Our new neighborhood was filled with kids in the same age bracket as our children, so we thought they would be blessed with playmates. Eventually they were; however, it took a while for our kids to feel welcome. I can remember more than one occasion when my children would come into the house sobbing because the neighborhood clique had rejected them in some way. My mother's heart experienced the pain right along with them.

Did you know that Jesus Christ suffered rejection? Isaiah 53:3 (NLT) says, "He was despised and rejected—a man of sorrows, acquainted with bitterest grief. We turned our backs on him and look the other way when he went by. He was despised, and we did not care."

What kind of people would knowingly be responsible for Jesus' pain? Would you believe it was those who actually should have been the closest to him? A classic example is found in the thirteenth chapter of Matthew. Here we see that the folks in Jesus' hometown of Nazareth were some of the first to make derisive comments when he spoke in the synagogue. In fact the very ones who had watched Jesus grow up were so offended by his profound teachings and astounding claims that they drove him out of town and tried to push him over a cliff. (Is it any wonder that Jesus was so impressed with the centurion's understanding and faith in Matthew 8?) This is the town where Jesus' immediate family still resided; yet, we are told that Jesus did very few miracles there because of the deep unbelief among the town's folk.

I don't believe there is any worse emotional pain than being rejected by family and friends—those to whom you have opened up and become most vulnerable. Jesus certainly experienced that type of rejection.

As we read on, we find three of Jesus' closest buddies were the cause of more emotional pain. Peter, a very loyal disciple and friend of Jesus, along with James and John, rejected Jesus by continually falling asleep in the Garden of Gethsemane. At that time, Jesus' heart was aching with sorrow over what he knew was about to happen, and he longed for their support. Then Peter went one step further by totally disowning Jesus when

> "Jesus understands rejection...he lived it."

the pressure was on. Later, of course, he was remorseful about his behavior and he wept bitterly. But, the fact still remains that he rejected Jesus when he feared for his own safety.

There should be no doubt in your mind that Jesus understands rejection. He lived it...and died experiencing the ultimate rejection of the Father on our behalf. His exact words were "My God, My God, why have you forsaken me?" Matthew 27:46 (NIV). Thank God, we do not have to experience the ultimate rejection of separation from the Father as Jesus did that day on the cross if we only accept God's free gift of eternal life offered to us through Jesus Christ. *[NOTE: If you still struggle with that, go back and review the first chapter of this book.]*

What can we learn from Jesus about handling rejection and heartache? First, Jesus didn't try to control another person's behavior. He didn't demand or force anyone to treat him differently than they were. Jesus didn't complain. Often, he remained quiet when his heart was probably aching. Isaiah 53:7 (NLT) states, "He was oppressed and treated harshly, yet he never said a word."

Secondly, Jesus recognized that his heavenly Father could provide what his earthly family and friends could not. (See Hebrews 13:5.) We, too, can always count on God to be there for us. He will never leave us or forsake us, no matter how rough the going gets.

Spiritual Pain

As your relationship with God increases and your faith is tested and strengthened, you may often feel some "spiritual growing pains." Don't be dismayed if you do, because the results are well worth it...and you're in good company!

There are a number of examples of spiritual growing pains in the Bible. Probably the best known is the story of Abraham and Isaac. Abraham had a close relationship with God, and there was no doubt about the love God had for Abraham. But God tested Abraham by stretching his faith to the limit with this request, "Take your son, your only son, Isaac, whom you love so much,... and sacrifice him as a burnt offering" (Genesis 22:2 NLT). Abraham could have balked at the request, but he didn't. The Bible tells us that he got up early and made preparations to carry out God's request. Abraham passed the test with flying colors and was blessed tremendously because of his obedience.

Let's face it. Everyone faces trials and times of testing. We may not always respond as graciously and obediently as Abraham and Isaac did. Sometimes we may even feel like we just can't endure the pain another minute, and we find ourselves being pulled into the pit of depression. God addresses those times in his Word as well.

According to Isaiah 43:1-2, it's not a matter of *if* you will experience trials in life, but rather *when.* Rest assured, though, that whenever you encounter them, they will not get the upper hand. With God's help you will "pass through" them unharmed. That should encourage you in knowing that your trials won't go on forever and that you have God's promise of protection as you go through them.

Learning From The Pain

One of my precious grandchildren, Brandon, is a high-functioning autistic child. Among his favorite things to do is to help in the kitchen. When he was about six years old, his mom and I were baking cookies for Christmas. We had just taken a pan of freshly baked cookies from the oven and set them on the counter when some interruption occurred—I don't remember exactly what it was. While we were otherwise occupied, Brandon quietly pulled a chair up to the counter so that he could smell the cookies up close. In the process, he laid his arms across the hot cookie sheet, which left noticeable burns. It was some time later when we realized what had happened because Brandon didn't complain a bit. You see, some children on the autism spectrum have very high pain thresholds. Brandon happens to be one of them, and he did not realize the danger because he was not aware of the pain.

Pain might seem like a bad thing, but pain has its place in the order of things. If we can't feel pain, we might be in harms way and not realize it.

God's Word offers us further insight regarding the things that cause pain in our lives and how it *can* be helpful. Rather than perceiving the pain as detrimental, we can actually use the pain to help us achieve new heights in our relationship with God.

> "Pain helps us achieve new heights with God."

In 1 Peter 4 verses 12-13, we are told not to be surprised if our faith is tested. Rather, we are to rejoice as God is revealed to us more and more. The periods of testing can shape us in the image of Jesus himself.

Psalm 42:11 encourages us not to be downcast or saddened when problems arise. Rather, we are to let hope and trust in God pull us back up.

According to Isaiah 40:31 we are to wait on the Lord rather than run out ahead of God and try to find the answers on our own. This is good advice no matter what the source of our pain is. God uses the eagle as a unique example of how we can weather the storms of life in the Isaiah passage. An eagle doesn't appear to be bothered by violent winds that bring threatening weather. In fact, it's been reported that when eagles sense the winds of a storm coming, they lift right into them head-on letting the storm winds lift them to new heights. Likewise, when problems threaten to push us down, we are to let God lift us to new heights as we put our trust in him.

Psalm 103:1-5 lists a number of reasons why we should be uplifted when we think of all the things God has done and continues to do for us. I challenge you to take time to speak this passage aloud the first thing every morning for one week. What a way to start the day!!

PSALM 103:1-5:
"I bless the holy name of God with all my heart.
Yes, I will bless the Lord and not forget the glorious things He does for me.
He forgives all my sins.
He heals me.
He ransoms me from hell.
He surrounds me with lovingkindness and tender mercies.
He fills my life with good things!
My youth is renewed like the eagle's!"(TLB)[3]

Chapter Five

God, I Think I'm Dying!

At this point in the exercise program, it's not uncommon to begin questioning whether the whole process is worth it. On the one hand, you probably recognize that you have gleaned at least some new insight from the examples of Jesus—things like how to clothe yourself spiritually, how to exercise the faith given to you, and how to deal with different types of pain along the way. But on the other hand, perhaps you feel you have gained little ground in becoming personally shaped in the image of Christ. After all, Jesus was the epitome of compassion, understanding, kindness, gentleness, wisdom, love, unselfishness—and the list goes on. Did I hear you say, "I'm not anywhere near that goal. Sometimes it just seems hopeless." Then, let me encourage you. Don't stop now—instead, we're going to step up the intensity! So, set your face like flint and let's continue the trek of becoming more like Christ. The best way to do that is to take an honest look at where you are now. Then, you can focus on getting to where you want to be—a true reflection of Jesus Christ!

Try This Revealing Exercise!

Monitor your thoughts for a day or even a smaller segment of time such as an hour. Keep a tally of the number of times you find yourself being self-focused. Below are some possible signs that reveal the "I" syndrome. Do any of these statements describe you? Be honest!!

- ❖ I find myself thinking often about problems I have.
- ❖ I'm usually the topic of my conversations with others.
- ❖ I feel tension rising within me when things don't go my way.
- ❖ My charge card bill reveals that I spend more on myself than anything else.
- ❖ Selfish motives prompt me to do the right thing for the wrong reason.
- ❖ How I will benefit personally often influences my decision on a matter.
- ❖ It bothers me when I cannot control a situation.
- ❖ I complain about physical ailments often.
- ❖ I am easily offended.

I'll let you in on a secret. I spent many years not even aware of the fact that I was engulfed in so many selfish thoughts. Maybe you are not conscious of them in yourself, either. Even if we are trying to do the right thing, our motive and focus is often on ourselves. We hear ourselves saying, "*I'm* going to try to do better…" –or "*I'm* trying to be more like Jesus." In your private prayer time, I encourage you to ask God to reveal your selfish nature to you. Perhaps you, like me, will be amazed at what you learn about yourself.

Still, we should not despair. God does not point out our weaknesses and then abandon us, but instead gives us some solid sources of help. God's help comes in the form of clear instruction and guidance in the Word.

I invite you to read Mark 8:34-35. What does Jesus say are the requirements for discipleship? First of all, we are to deny ourselves; then, we are to take up our cross and follow Jesus. It is noteworthy that Jesus did not give these requirements only to his twelve disciples. Verse 34 says that he called the crowd to him along with the disciples. These words of wisdom were intended for all who would believe.

What does it mean to "deny yourself?" Personally, I don't believe Jesus meant doing without or refusing to give some *thing* to yourself. For example, many people deny themselves a piece of dessert if they are dieting. But usually the reason they do is still self-focused—they want to lose weight in order to look more attractive. The attention is still on self. To deny one's self, I believe, means to disregard one's own interests altogether. In other words, don't even stop to consider yourself. Get your eyes off yourself and what you want, think or feel. The New Living Translation puts it this way— "put aside your selfish ambitions" (Mark 9:34). Instead, turn your eyes upon Jesus and to the needs of others. That's a tough order to fill, isn't it? Human nature and selfish desires are bound to surface at least occasionally, no matter how hard we try.

To "carry our cross" is another figure of speech that is often misinterpreted to mean putting up with some kind of irritation in life, perhaps for the sake of becoming humble. Usually, this kind of thinking brings about the opposite result of humility. If we look at bearing the cross as an irritant, it becomes so easy to fall into the "poor me" trap. Again, the focus turns inward to self rather than outward toward the people of God.

What, then, did Jesus mean by this statement? *The Expositor's Bible Commentary* paints a picture of a man, already condemned, required to carry his cross on the way to the place of execution, as Jesus was required to do.[1] Although the cross was a Roman method of execution, it was well known to the Jews of Jesus' day. Certainly the Christians in Rome were acquainted with it. The cross was the symbol for death. Therefore, to "bear the cross" means a death is about to take place. The sinful self has to die daily, or following Jesus is not possible. Just as Jesus took our sin to the cross to be crucified, so we too must crucify our sin-sick flesh. Without that death, there can be no new life.

> "Without death, there can be no new life."

Mark expounds on that thought in the next several verses. Whoever chooses to save his life *(by not allowing one's sinful flesh to die)* will lose it *(by ultimately not inheriting eternal life)*. However, the opposite is true as well. Whoever loses his life *(dies to sin)* in order to remain faithful to Jesus will truly live eternally with him.

Included in the Bible is a letter known as Colossians. It was written by the apostle Paul to the early believers in the city of Colosse in Asia Minor, which is now called Turkey. In the third chapter of this letter Paul lists some specifics that were problems in their culture, and they are the same things that are common today. He mentions rampant sexual immorality, anger, rage, greed, losing control of one's temper, jealousy, spreading untruths about others and inappropriate language.

According to this passage, the "old self" must die. Our sinful flesh must be crucified; it must die daily. Notice the influence of our mind on this action in verse 2: "Set your minds on things above, not on earthly things." God is to be the center of our lives. Without assistance from God, there is no way we could "put to death" our old, sinful behavior when it threatens us *(verse 5)*. Saying "no" to wrong choices is not always easy, but it *is* possible if we completely surrender to the Father, just as Jesus did.

How is our sinful flesh "put to death?" Obviously, we cannot do it on our own. Our human nature and the thoughts and attitudes it typically produces are too strong for human willpower to resist. But by the power of the Holy Spirit *in* us, it is possible to overcome our human nature. First, we must make certain that we have invited Jesus into our heart. By prayer and a growing trust in him day by day, the Holy Spirit will increasingly give us the strength to do what is right. Over a period of time, the "old flesh" dies or is stripped away, and it becomes increasingly replaced with many new Christ-like characteristics—the new wardrobe we discovered in chapter two of this book.

Sometimes we make an attempt to become "the new self" without our former self first dying. Jesus gave several examples of trying to mix old with new in Matthew 9:16-17. What does he say are the results?

Obviously, the "old" and "new" don't mix well. Jesus talked about putting new wine in old wine skins and patching old cloth with new cloth that has not been pre-shrunk. Both produce less than satisfactory results. Similarly, we can't have both and expect to succeed.

My Personal Revelation

A number of years ago I experienced a recurring dream. The scene of the dream was always the same—a house with a small front room jammed with two distinctly different styles of furniture. In the dream I always attempted to rearrange the furnishings to get everything to fit together properly and be aesthetically pleasing, but I could never accomplish it. The room always appeared crowded and in extreme disarray. There was a long hallway with stairs leading to another room in the back of the house. This room was bursting with light and totally void of all furnishings. It was an area I knew I would like to experience, yet I seldom went back to it since my concentration was always on the front room.

After several years of having the same dream, it finally occurred to me to ask God for wisdom regarding its meaning. He granted that request almost immediately. The room, you see, was me. One type of furnishings represented the desires and passions of my fleshly nature. The other style stood for the Christ-like qualities I was striving to attain. God showed me that I had been attempting to mix the "new" in with the "old." All this was taking place in the most visible area of my life—the front room. I was trying to experience the new qualities without allowing the old lifestyle to be "put to death." I knew it was possible to go back into the inner chambers of my spirit to experience God's Holy Sprit who was waiting to provide cleansing, warmth and refreshing solitude, but I seldom took the opportunity. I was too busy trying to clean and rearrange on my own. "Self" had failed to die.

What are your own personal struggles with the "killing of your flesh?" I believe God often uses circumstance in our lives to help kill our flesh—experiences like people whom we can't control; people that attempt to control us; circumstances beyond our control that disappoint or upset us. Perhaps you have noticed other flesh-killers in your own life. Are you allowing your flesh to be put to death? Are you ready to "die" daily? Only YOU can answer the question.

Chapter Six

What's My Heart Rate?

When I started using the treadmills at our local YMCA I needed a lesson on how to use the electronic display panel at the front of the machine. There were all kinds of gadgets available to monitor my time spent walking, the distance traveled, the speed and even the calories I burned during my workout. *(Incidentally, it's amazing how few calories are burned from tons of effort!)* I found out that the machine could display my heart rate at any given point if I placed my hands on the handgrips in front of me. On some of the machines you can even use a preprogrammed option, and the treadmill adjusts the incline to keep your heart rate at a certain predetermined level.

I believe it is just as essential to take inventory of our heart as we exercise spiritually. We should take time periodically to examine our spiritual heart to see if our inner attitude coincides with our outward behavior. If our heart is not healthy, our actions don't stand a chance in the long run. Even if we appear to be doing the right things, it's easy to become frustrated if our heart isn't truly functioning for God.

How can you determine if your heart is beating properly? What is it that strengthens your heart so that you are more efficient, productive and loving in your Christian walk? Let's find out.

The Heart, Defined

Physically speaking, the heart is a hollow muscular organ, which keeps our blood circulating throughout our bodies. Its job is mind boggling, really—it's what keeps us alive. Our aerobic activities (or lack of activities) directly influence the strength of our heart. Through an understanding of heart rate, we are capable of developing an aerobic fitness routine to safely improve our cardiovascular fitness.

When the Bible refers to the heart, generally it is talking about something other than the physical organ. The word heart came to stand for "the center of a person's moral, intellectual and spiritual life."[1] The heart, in this sense, lies deep within a person and is responsible for shaping one's will, emotions and true character. In essence, it is what keeps our spirit operating, just as the human heart is necessary to keep the body functioning.

The healthiness of one's spiritual heart is not readily visible to the human eye. But just as medical professionals have ways of determining if the physical heart is healthy so, too, God has the ability to see into our spiritual heart and diagnose any malfunctions. He sees the secrets of every heart.[2] Ouch! When we are hiding a secret sin, the last thing we want is to be probed, searched or convicted by God.

The Bible is quite descriptive about the heart. Jeremiah 17:9-10 tells us that the human heart is deceitful beyond cure. The very core and lifeblood of our being is infected with a terminal disease—sin. It's a killer, all right. The good news is that Jesus is the one who took the brunt of our deadly disease. His death and resurrection brought the healing we need. Ezekiel 11:18-19 tells us that God offers to remove our terminally ill heart of stone and replace it with a tender, responsive heart that beats for Jesus. Now that's my kind of heart transplant! And it doesn't even require a stay in the hospital!

The sixth chapter of Luke's gospel adds insight to the whole issue of the heart. Luke points out in verse 44 that just as a tree is identified by it's fruit, whatever is going on inside each of us at the root is what will eventually make it's appearance. We may be able to "fool *some* of the people *some* of the time,"[3] but eventually the true nature of our hearts will be revealed through our actions and speech. (See Matthew 15:18-19.) A heart that is not beating for God becomes diseased with all sorts of evil thoughts leading to murder, adultery, theft, sexual immorality, lying or slander. But, a heart that is rooted and grounded in Jesus is healthy and will bring forth "good fruit."

God is continually searching your heart. God alone has the ability to truly penetrate and examine what is in the heart. It's possible to give God lip service all the while your heart may be far from him. But God knows that; he can't be fooled. God's purpose is not to catch us in sin and condemn us, but to cleanse those sins from us by the powerful washing of Jesus' redemptive blood. As we truly accept the sacrifice that Jesus made in payment for our sins, our grimy, calloused heart is replaced with a heart that is spiritually alive, open to God, and clean.

> "God alone can truly penetrate and examine the heart."

With the psalmist, we can come to God in prayer asking for that cleansing and purification process to take place in our own heart.[4]

Your Heart's Desire—Love!

We all have one thing in common when it comes to the basic need of the heart. What is it? It's a craving, longing, desire or need to be loved. God made us that way so that we could be ready recipients of his love.

But along with that desire comes the notion that we have to do something to earn or bring about that love—to be good, desirable, lovable, alluring, charming, attractive, etc. That way, we feel we *deserve* the love. Where do you think that concept comes from? I call it the "Santa Syndrome." We are taught from little on that if we are good there will be a reward. Sad to say, charming our way to love may work as the world defines it—at least for a while—but then comes the feeling that something is missing, and off we go once again in search of something to satisfy that deep longing or need within us.

The truth is nothing will ever completely satisfy that craving within until we open up our hearts to receive God's love. God's love is different than human love. Even the greatest human love is severely limited compared to God's love. Often, it is difficult for us to accept God's love because we try to limit God to what we think love is according to our shallow understanding.

The Bible clearly teaches that God's love is unlimited (*has no boundaries*) and unconditional (*not dependent on what we are, do, or deserve*). Why is that such a difficult thing to perceive? To help you understand let's look at some of the differences between conditional and unconditional love.

Conditional love is based on performance. It's the attitude that in order to be loved, I must do something to earn it. When I do good things I feel loved, but when I do unacceptable things I feel rejected and cut off from the source of love. Conditional love means I'm in constant need of feedback from other people to prove that I am valuable and loved. Since love is based on what I do, I give love only out of a desire to be loved, not just for the sake of loving another person.

Quite the opposite, being loved unconditionally is not based on my performance, actions or attitude. I don't have to do anything to deserve the love; in fact, I feel love no matter what I've done. I never feel rejected because nothing can separate me from this love. I feel accepted and loved at all times without having to be told constantly. Since love is not based on what I do or what someone else does, I am free to love and be loved at any time.

> **"God's love is *never* dependent on what we do."**

God's love is *never* dependent on what we do; yet somehow we tend to be fooled into thinking that we can earn "brownie points" with God by our behavior. We must remember that we can never be good enough to earn God's love. His love is continuous and unconditional for everyone that will receive it. God loves us simply because he IS love (1 John 4:8). God can't help but love you and me!

It's easy for some people to believe that God loved "the world," but they have trouble believing that God loves *them*. Do you believe that God loves *you*? Do you know that if you were the only person on earth, Jesus still would have suffered death and separation from God for just YOU? That's how precious you are to God.

Falling "In Love" . . . With God!

It is possible to fall head-over-heels in love with God. Is that a new concept for you? Remember, love is a relationship. God loves you. If you are not consciously aware of it, or if you don't *receive* it and return the love, you won't be able to enjoy it. So go ahead... choose to fall in love with God. The results may astound you!

What generally happens when you fall in love? Think of your first experience with falling in love. Most of us probably trace our first "heart throb" to our teen years or perhaps even earlier. As I recall my first puppy love happened in grade school. The young man who stole my heart back then was constantly on my mind. I could scarcely think of anything else. I wanted to spend every waking moment in his presence. I longed to talk to him and tell him about my feelings, yet I didn't know what to say. I'm sure my feelings for him were no secret to those around me, though. It was evident in my behavior, not to mention the big smile on my face!

Should my love relationship with Jesus bring an even greater response? As I continue to grow in my intimacy with him, I find myself wanting to spend time in his presence. I long to find out more about him. I read books that give me insight into his nature, and I listen regularly to people who can tell me more about him. I want to do the things I know will please him. I am courageous enough to talk to him regularly, even though it seemed awkward at first. Now, not only do I enjoy talking *to* him, I love to talk *about* him. Nothing gives me greater pleasure than telling others how great God really is!

Some people have told me they have difficulty thinking of themselves as having an intimate love relationship with God. However, throughout the Bible the imagery exists. In the Old Testament Israel is referred to as the bride, the wife of the Lord (Isaiah 54:5). In the New Testament, Christ's deep love and commitment to the body of believers is compared to the marriage covenant. (See Ephesians 5:22-32.)

Check Your Pulse Regularly!

Love is expressive, but we can't give away what we do not have. We must first accept the gift of love from our Lord before we truly and consistently are able to "pass it on." Continue to reflect on God's love for you and check the pulse of your love for God as you study these additional scriptures:

- ❖ John 3:16 – God's love is so great that he gave his only unique Son that we might be saved.
- ❖ John 12:1-8 – Mary expressed unrestrained love for Jesus. Do you?
- ❖ 1 John 4:7-21 – Love reaches out through each of us.
- ❖ John 13:34-35 – Loving is God's "new" commandment.
- ❖ Galatians 5:22 – Love is the first "fruit" that is produced in us by the Spirit.
- ❖ 1 John 4:18 – Perfect love casts out fear.
- ❖ 1 Peter 4:8 – Love covers a multitude of sins.
- ❖ Romans 8:35-39 – Love links us permanently to God!

Chapter Seven

The Importance of Diet

Proper nutrition is a very important part of any exercise program. It makes no sense to devote yourself to physical fitness through rigorous exercise and then waste all the efforts by feasting on the wrong foods. There's a lot of truth in the old saying, "You are what you eat." We could probably sum up most of our eating habits in one or more of the following categories. Which one(s) are characteristic of you?

❖ Sorry, I'm not hungry.

❖ I'm starved, but I'm trying to stick to this new diet.

❖ In a hurry...! Fast food, that's for me!

❖ Rushed or not, I'm a "junk-food-aholic" through and through.

❖ Give me balance— "three squares" a day, please.

❖ I'm a "nibbler."

❖ Oh how I love a good meal in a relaxing atmosphere where I can savor *every* bite!

❖ I'm going to keep eating until I'm thoroughly satisfied!

Food For Thought — Your "Spiritual" Diet

We grow up with the knowledge that our bodies require food and water to survive. Without fluid intake dehydration occurs. If a person goes for a long period of time without fluid it can even cause death. By the same token if we don't eat our body decreases in size and in strength. We become malnourished and more susceptible to disease.

Often we fail to realize that our spirits need daily nourishment. Spiritual food is essential for spiritual healthiness just as physical food is necessary to sustain physical life. Ask yourself the following questions:

- ❖ What are your symptoms of spiritual hunger?
- ❖ In what way do you react to your spiritual hunger?
- ❖ Do any of the categories listed above describe your spiritual hunger and eating habits? If so, which one(s)?
- ❖ What "spiritual food" do you take in?
- ❖ Is your spiritual hunger satisfied or are you still hungry and thirsty?

Satisfy Your Hunger With The Right Bread!

The sixth chapter of John begins with the famous story of Jesus feeding a huge mass of people with a small amount of food from a young boy's lunch. Jesus knew that the folks who had been crowding around him were drawn to him by his miraculous healings and his intriguing words. He took full advantage of a teaching moment and gave them great advice regarding their spiritual diet. He told them to spend their time and energy seeking the eternal life that He could give them, not for miraculous appearances of food for the body.

When Jesus referred to himself as the "bread of life" he was drawing on a rich symbol of Jewish life. Bread played an important role in Israel's worship. It was an essential part of the sacrifices offered during the celebration of Pentecost (Leviticus 23:17). Also, twelve loaves of unleavened bread were placed before the Lord in the tabernacle each week to symbolize God's presence with the twelve tribes (Exodus 25:30). [1]

Jesus told his followers not to labor for food that would perish but rather to seek the food that would have lasting qualities (John 6:27). How does one acquire that food? Jesus was asked the same question in verse 28. They wanted to know what they could do to please God enough to gain this "eternal life." But what does Jesus say is required of us in verse 29? Only believe! We are directed to the "gift of God" that can only be obtained through Jesus. Perhaps they were missing the key word—gift. So often we, too, are guilty of trying to *do* something to earn the bread rather than just receive what God offers us as a free gift.

This group of people could have been from the "show me" state of Missouri *(where I reside!)* because they immediately responded, "Show us a miraculous sign if you want us to believe." *(As if they needed more proof than what they had already seen!)* Then they reminded Jesus of how God miraculously sustained their ancestors through their wilderness travels by sending manna from heaven each morning (Exodus 16). However, Jesus quickly pointed out to them that manna was provided by God to satisfy *physical* hunger, not *spiritual* hunger. To them, believing meant acceptance of Jesus' competence based on his miracles. To Jesus, it meant trusting him *without* the evidence of miracles.

When Jesus referred to himself as "the *true* bread from heaven" (John 6:32-33) the Jews didn't waste a moment to mutter to themselves, "Who does he think he is? Isn't this just Jesus, the son of Joseph? What is this business about coming down from heaven?"

At the conclusion of this passage Jesus makes yet another mystifying statement: "Unless you eat the flesh of the Son of Man and drink his blood, you have no life in you" (verse 53). What a perplexing thing for Jesus to say. Yet, these ideas would be quite normal to anyone brought up in ancient sacrifice. The sacrificial animal was very seldom burned entirely. Usually only a token part was burned on the altar. Part of the flesh was given to the priests as a bonus, and part to the worshipper to make a feast for himself and his friends within the temple. When people rose from such a feast they went out, as they believed, literally god-filled.[2] When Jesus made the statement about eating his flesh and drinking his blood, he was making the point that intellectual belief is not enough. He calls each of us to go further than that. We are to base our entire lives upon Jesus. To eat and drink Jesus is to allow him to permeate our very soul.

> "Intellectual belief is not enough."

Have you made the decision to take Jesus into *every* aspect of your life? Do you have a passionate, ever-increasing yearning for a close, intimate relationship with Jesus? Do you hunger for more of him? Or are you "lukewarm?" Are you afraid to be set on fire for the Lord for fear you will be called a fanatic? So many of us who call ourselves Christians experience very little hunger, thirst and passion for our Lord and Savior. Is Christ "in you?" Are you "in Christ?" (See 2 Corinthians 5:17; Romans 8:1.)

Having accepted the "gift" of faith to believe in Jesus as your Savior, can you be sure that you will live eternally? If you are not certain, read John 3:16. Also read again John 6:40; and verses 47 and 54. Jesus repeatedly says that whoever believes in him has everlasting life. He is the living bread that came down from heaven. "The bread I give is my flesh, which I give for the life of the world. If anyone eats of this bread *(believes)* and drinks this blood *(takes in and accepts that Jesus' shed blood was the atoning sacrifice for one's sins),* he will live forever."

How is your spiritual appetite? Do you eat until you are satisfied? If you are filling up on things of the world (personal pleasures, material goods, etc.) you will have little appetite for spiritual food. The problem is you will never satisfy your hunger with things of this world. Jesus says that if you fill up on the "bread of life" you won't ever hunger. The perpetual dissatisfaction and discontent you once felt will be gone. In its place will be real lasting peace, contentment and a deep, satisfying joy! So go ahead and eat all you want. You can never get too much!

"Living Water"—The Thirst Quencher!

As I mentioned earlier in this chapter, my home is in Missouri. One thing is certain—it gets extremely hot in the summer months. After my husband has been outside mowing our lawn, it's not unusual for him to come into the house with his lips and tongue coated from dehydration. The first thing he does when he enters the house is to get a huge glass of water to replace the fluids he has lost out in the heat. I'm sure there have been times when you have experienced extreme thirst like that.

Did you know that you could become spiritually parched as well? It is common to have high and low points in your faith walk and, yes, there are times when you may feel bone dry. You may even cry out, "Where are you, God?" This type of spiritual dehydration can have serious consequences if left unattended. Just like the body needs water to survive, so we are destined to die spiritually of dehydration if we don't drink "living water."

There is a very familiar story in the fourth chapter of John's gospel about a woman from Samaria. The Jews in Jesus' day typically did not mingle at all with the Samaritans. Besides that, it was considered disreputable for a Jewish teacher like Jesus to speak to a woman in public. In this story, Jesus went right through Samaria on his way to Galilee. Weary from traveling, Jesus sat down beside a well to rest a bit. Apparently he had no way to get water from the well, so when a woman from Samaria came to draw some water he struck up a conversation with her, asking her for a drink.

The Samaritan woman said, "Why do you ask me for a drink?" Jesus aroused her curiosity even more when he told her she must not know who was asking her for a drink or she would be asking *him* for a drink instead, and he would have given her living water. The key words here are the same ones we have seen in other applications—*gift* from God…, *ask*…, and *receive*.

Obviously, the Samaritan women did not know what Jesus meant by living water. Verse 15 indicates that she was looking at the physical aspect of his offer to quench her thirst. She wanted something to permanently satisfy her physical and material needs. Jesus was attempting to get her to understand that being "filled up" with God would be the only thing that could really quench an unsatisfied thirst. In the final words of their conversation (verses 25-26), Jesus revealed his true identity to her. This is one of few times when Jesus actually says he is the long-awaited Messiah.

"The Spirit becomes like a stream within the believer."

Jesus talks about the living water again in John 7:37-39. This passage clearly states that the "living water" is the Holy Spirit, received by those who believe in Jesus. The Spirit becomes like a stream within the believer, ever flowing and ever satisfying. It's the same Spirit that Jesus promised to give us all if we love him and obey his commands. (See John 14:15-17.) This Spirit comes to take up residence within us. Our bodies become the temple or dwelling place of the Spirit (1 Corinthians 6:19).

There is a song that says, "I've got a river of life flowing out of me, makes the lame to walk and the blind to see, opens prison doors, sets the captives free; I've got a river of life flowing out of me."[3] Do you have this supply of living water flowing from within you? I encourage you to read and study the following passages to give you further understanding into the living water of the Spirit that is within you.

Romans 8:9-11 emphasizes that if you have taken Jesus Christ into every area of your life (drink), you belong to him and he is in you.

In Mark 1:6-8, John the baptizer stated emphatically to his followers that there was one coming after him who would do more than just baptize with water. That one is Jesus, who "baptizes with the Holy Spirit." He is the one who fills us from head to toe with the refreshing living water.

Luke 11:11-13 states in Jesus' own words that if earthly fathers know how to give good gifts, how much more will our Heavenly Father give the Holy Spirit to those who ask. All you need to do is ask God, and the Holy Spirit will be given to you!

If you have accepted the fact that Jesus Christ, God's only unique Son, loved you so much that he paid for your eternal salvation with his blood on the cross, there is never any reason to doubt that he will fill you up to the brim with his Spirit. The Spirit provides the power within you to walk a victorious, loving Christian life. So go ahead, walk in victory!

Are you hungry? Then "taste and see that the Lord is good!" (Psalm 24:8). Seek God earnestly; praise him, and your soul will be satisfied with the richest of foods. If you are thirsty, God will pour out his water on you and your offspring. Blessed are those who hunger and thirst for righteousness, for they will be filled!

Chapter Eight

The Jogging Path

Your exercise program wouldn't be complete without a good healthy jaunt. Okay, maybe you're not ready to take off running, but you can certainly handle a nice walk! Ready to put on your walking shoes and begin? Okay! Well, wait a minute.... Where are you going? Where is your life leading you?

If you are like me, there are times when your life is like a treadmill—I am walking, walking, walking, and never getting anywhere. On the other hand, I may experience a relatively calm season, which puts me in mind of a leisurely stroll the park, hand-in-hand with my husband. Then suddenly life becomes a rat race, and I feel like a hamster spinning aimlessly in one of those enclosed balls that runs into everything in its path!

Where Are You Headed?

As you walk, run or spin your way through life, what's at the "finish line" for you? The best God has to offer us as we complete our earthly race is eternal life. Is that what's in store for you? Many people don't really know for sure what is going to happen to them when they die. Can anyone ever *really* be sure of what is at the finish line?

The late Dr. D. James Kennedy, founder and senior pastor of Coral Ridge Ministries, was known for his bold approach to evangelism by asking some direct and thought-provoking questions:

❖ Have you come to a place in your spiritual walk where you can say *for certain* that you would go to heaven when you die?

❖ Suppose you were to die today and God asks you, "Why should I let you into my heaven?" How would you respond?

To the first question it is possible to say a resounding "Yes!" There is a way you can be certain that heaven awaits you as you cross the finish line! But make sure your confidence is based on the truth of scripture. That's where the second question comes in.

I can't begin to count the number of times I have heard people respond to these questions with a false sense of security in their own merit. Common statements are, "I may not be perfect, but God knows I try to do the right thing." "I'm as good (or better) as the next guy." "Yes, I believe I'll get to heaven. I don't think God would refuse anyone who was trying to be good." But try as we might, we are never good enough to measure up to God's standard. Our righteous acts are like filthy rags in God's sight. (See Isaiah 64:6.) If we could muster up our own right standing with God, there would have been no need for Jesus to die for our sins. The fact is that we cannot be "right" with God on our on accord. It is simply through belief in God's act of love through Jesus that we are credited as righteous before God. The fourth chapter of Romans offers an excellent explanation of how we receive that status. Verse 5 of that chapter sums it up with this simple statement, "People are declared righteous because of their faith, *not* because of their work." *(Emphasis mine.)*

Identifying The Right Path

None of us want to think about death being an end of our existence, nor do we want to even consider that we could exist in a place of torment being cut off from God's mercy forever. Our ultimate goal and desire is to be with our Lord and our loved ones in heaven throughout eternity. We all are pretty clear about the goal. Seldom do you hear anyone say they do not want to end up in heaven. But if our righteous acts—our "good deeds"—do not measure up to God's standard, then what does? What is the correct path? How do we know if we are on the right path? How do we find it?

Jesus identifies the way for us over and over again in the Bible. One of the first verses of the Bible I memorized as a child was John 3:16—"For God so loved the world that he gave his only Son, so that everyone who believes in him will not perish but have eternal life." Simply said, we must believe.

The apostle Paul states it just as clearly in Romans 10:9-10 (NIV). "For if you confess with your mouth that Jesus is Lord and believe in your heart that God raised him from the dead, you will be saved. For it is by believing in your heart that you are made right with God, and it is by confessing with your mouth that you are saved."

The pathway between man and God, once severed by sin, has been restored through Jesus. He is the perfect bridge that brings sinful man back into fellowship with God. William Barclay, in his *Daily Study Bible Series of the Gospel of John*, gives the following example:

> "The pathway has been restored through Jesus."

Suppose you are in a strange town and need directions. The person you have asked for directions says, "Take the first right and then the second on the left. Cross the square and go past the church, take the third on the right and the road you want is the fourth on the left." Chances are you will be lost before you get half way. But, suppose the person you ask says, "Come. I'll take you there." In that case the person to us *is* the way. He does not only give advice and directions. He takes us by the hand and leads us; he strengthens us and guides us personally every step of the way.[1]

Jesus does exactly the same thing for each of us. He does not want us to lose our way. He is our constant companion, going the extra mile to make certain we are gently nudged to stay on the right path. The problem is we don't always take hold of Jesus' hand and let him lead. We are like little children who are eager to run out ahead and explore the territory, even though there may be dangers lurking.

Let's Take A Walk!

The Bible is full of wisdom about how to continue the walk with Jesus. But we don't always like where the path leads us. Often we find ourselves at crossroads that require decisions on our part. Choices have to be made that are not always easy or comfortable for us. Furthermore, there are obstacles along the path that can send us in the opposite direction of where we should be going. Let's identify some obstacles and see how we can avoid them in our own personal walk.

Psalm 1:1 gives some great advice—"don't walk in the counsel of the wicked or stand in the way of sinners or sit in the seat of mockers." Well, that's an easy one...or is it? We are not to take on the ways, actions or speech of the ungodly. Ever criticize or mock how another believer or church body expresses their worship to God— ever done that? Ever display nervous embarrassment or rolled your eyes back when someone freely talks about Jesus in a public setting? Ever been tempted to use God's name as an expletive in an effort to fit in with the crowd? ...or when you hit your finger with a hammer? You are blessed indeed if you don't even consider going down that path. But if you find yourself tempted to stray, make a conscious decision to take the high road.

> "Take the high road."

Colossians 3:5-10 mentions the places we used to walk before we were raised with Christ and began setting our minds are things above. We used to walk according to our earthly nature—sexual sins, lust, shameful desire, greed for things in this life, anger, rage, malicious behavior, slander, filthy language, to mention a few. Now we walk in the newness of life. Don't trip over those old habits any longer!

And another word of warning—don't let adversities become stumbling blocks in our path. Instead, see them as situations where God is teaching and guiding you. Isaiah 30:21 says, "Whether you turn to the right or to the left, your ears will hear a voice behind you saying, 'This is the way; walk in it.'" God's leading voice is never out of earshot if we but listen.

Is Your Pathway Well Lit?

My husband will be the first to admit that he is very direction-ally challenged. He struggles nearly every time he tries to find his way to a new place. Before the days of directional-aiding devices in automobiles and cell phones, it was even more of a problem. I can usually find my way anywhere in the daytime without much dif-ficulty, but at night it's a whole different story. Quite frankly, I just don't see well at night. If I don't have the sun to provide that sense of direction I can be led astray quite easily.

It is no less of a problem trying to find our way down the spiri-tual street if we are groping in darkness. Without light on the pathway, we are destined to stumble and fall. But our pathway doesn't have to be without light. There is a constant light source available to us.

Psalm 89:15 tells us that we are blessed when we walk in the light of God's presence. Where do we find that light that is so desperately needed? Psalm 119:105 gives the answer, "Your word is a lamp to guide my feet and a light for my path." Turn on the flashlight God has given you so you can see where you are going! The light of God's word brings enlightenment and keeps us from tripping over any obstacles that may be on life's path.

The gospel-writer, John, records a conversation Jesus had with a group of unbelievers. Jesus' words were, "I am the light of the world. If you follow Me, you won't have to walk in darkness, be-cause you will have the light that leads to life" (John 8:12 NLT).

Light always overcomes darkness. If we remain in God's pres-ence, we can't help but be in the light. In God there is no darkness. God's Word provides a constant source of light for each of us. As we walk in that light, we find fellowship with Jesus and with one another, and we will be blessed.

The Race Is On!

The writers of several New Testament books give us some pow-erful examples of running the race and the importance of staying on course. The Greek games in those times featured several sports, including chariot racing, horse racing, and foot racing, and these writers no doubt had those athletic events in mind when they spoke of a person's life as a race course to run.[2]

I invite you to look up the following passages that talk about the Christian's race. How do you picture the athlete described in each situation?

- ❖ Corinthians 9:24-27
- ❖ Hebrews 12:1-2
- ❖ 2 Timothy 4:7-8

Can't you just see the look of determination in the eyes of the first athlete? He's practicing strict self-control as he runs in such a way as to win the prize. He's headed straight for the goal with purpose in every step. He does not waver!

I picture the second athlete starting his long race with all kinds of essentials (at least in *his* mind!) strapped to his body. Trying to keep it all balanced on his shoulders is very distracting, not to mention how weighted down he feels. Then I see him begin to cast them aside, one by one—first the sack of fear and insecurity, then the box stuffed with materialism, next the little packets of worry, deceit and doubt. The lighter his load gets the easier it is to keep his eyes of the goal, the finish line—Jesus!

The last athlete is a winner, for sure! He fought the race fair and square and is nearing the finish line. He is remaining faithful right to the end. Once his foot is over that finish line the prize is his—a unique crown placed on him by God, himself!

Run your race to win! An athlete gives all for the sake of worldly recognition and a prize that has no real lasting value. In the apostle Paul's day, an athlete's training and discipline resulted in a "corruptible crown"—a laurel wreath that would soon wither away.[3] However, Christians who are faithful to the end of the race are promised a "crown" that is indestructible—that of eternal life and fellowship with God that will last forever. (See Revelation 2:10.)

> "Run your race to win!"

As our race is taking place, it's as if all the earlier heroes of faith (Hebrews 11) are seated in the stadium, watching our race and cheering us on.[4] We are instructed to drop everything that might weigh us down and run with perseverance. We are to "fix our eyes" on Jesus, the one who gives us faith and then continues to perfect it to the end; the one who supplies all the strength we'll ever need.

The apostle Paul recognized that strength when he made his final visit to Rome. The trip was not a pleasant experience for him, for it ended up in imprisonment. He could have been depressed and disappointed. He could have said, "God, why did you allow this to happen to me?" But instead of defeat, Paul tells his young pastoral friend, "I have fought the good fight, I have finished the race, I have kept the faith." Will you be able to say the same thing at the end of your race?

You're A Winner!

Look back at the questions at the beginning of this chapter. Hopefully, you can answer with confidence that heaven awaits you as you cross the finish line. You can be assured of eternal life with God because—

❖ you have acknowledged that you are a sinner;
❖ you recognize that the payment for sin is death (separation from God);
❖ you believe that Jesus paid the debt of your sin with his own blood sacrifice;
❖ you have accepted Jesus as your Savior and confessed it to other people; and
❖ your daily surrender to Jesus allows him to be Lord of your life, which is exemplified in acts of love and service to the people of God.

Yes, you can be certain of eternal life. Don't doubt it! Walk in victory proclaiming Jesus Christ as the way, the truth and the life.

Chapter Nine

Walking...and Talking:
An Exercise On Prayer

M ost of us are engaged in a moderately long walk through life. We would get pretty lonely if we didn't have someone to chat with along the way. Well, there is good news! We never have to walk the road alone. Throughout the Bible God has shown time and time again that he will not desert his people. Probably one of the most familiar references is in Hebrew 13:5 (NIV), "Never will I leave you, never will I forsake you." Furthermore, God has given us a unique way of staying in touch with him at all times—prayer.

What Is Prayer?

When my oldest grandson, Cameron, was just a little tyke, I had the frequent privilege of tucking him in bed for the night. Most of the time he liked to be the one to pray, but on one particular evening he asked me to say the prayer. As he and I knelt by the side of his bed I offered a prayer of thanksgiving for the blessings of the day and asked for God's protection over him as he slept. When I finished the prayer, Cameron curled up on the floor, knees to his chest, and remained unusually quiet. After a few moments of silence I gently placed my hand on his back and said, "Cameron, are you okay?" He answered, "Yes, gwamma... I'm just talkin' to God with my heart." That's probably the best definition of prayer I've ever heard! I didn't know what was on Cameron's heart that night, but it didn't matter—God knew.

Prayer is having a heart-to-heart talk with none other than the Creator of the universe! Did you ever stop to consider what an awesome privilege that is? The personal relationship we can each have with the almighty God was made possible by the death and resurrection of Jesus. Christ bridged the gap between God and man so that we have the freedom to talk to God whenever we want. It doesn't matter what age we are, where we are, or what is on our mind. Just like any other relationship, though, our relationship with God is strengthened through communication—which includes both talking and listening!

Hundreds of references to prayer fill the pages of the Bible, including the examples of Jesus himself in prayer. Some people stood with hands lifted up to God; others were so humbled by God's acknowledgment of them that they knelt down or laid on their faces before the Lord. Some prayed silently while others gave shouts of praise or cries of despair. Some prayed together in temples or homes; others preferred quiet communion with God.

There are many reasons for communicating with God. You can tell God how much you love him. You can give thanks for all the things God does. You can confess your sins and ask for forgiveness. You can ask for specific things, both for yourself and on behalf of others. Probably most important is to listen to what God has to say to you! Prayer is sharing one's self completely with God.

From "Baby Talk" To "Adult Conversation"

My granddaughter, Parker Anne, is a brilliant child. I'm not just saying that because she's my only granddaughter *(she came along after 3 grandsons)*. Her vocabulary is incredible; it always has been. She wasn't much past her first birthday when she started talking full sentences...*with* meaning! You could tell she thought things through. You could actually have a great conversation with her. I knew she was exceptional.

When most children begin to talk, they repeat things they hear even though they may not always know the meaning of what is said.

But as time goes on, they begin to formulate their own ideas and express their own personal thoughts in words. Some people use a lot of descriptive words as they speak. Others are able to state what they mean in just a matter of a few words. Either way, communication is unique to each person who is doing the communicating.

Our conversation with God develops in a similar way. For most of us it's a progressive thing. In the early stages of our relationship we feel most comfortable repeating something familiar like traditional prayers before meals or at bedtime. Soon, we start to venture out on our own in conversations with God. Our chats with God may be short and to the point, or we may find ourselves talking to God either audibly or in our thoughts for hours. Our prayers may be in words that we understand or they may be in "groans" that the Spirit gives us when we don't know what to say.[1] No matter how they sound to us or to anyone around us, each offered prayer is a unique conversation with God.

Places and Postures For Prayer

You can pray anywhere! In his well-known Sermon on the Mount (Matthew 5-7), Jesus points out the intimacy and personal nature of prayer as he invites us to pray "in secret." But, he talks also, about the power of gathering together with others to pray in agreement (Matthew 18:19-20). After Jesus' ascension, the apostles went back to Jerusalem and gathered for prayer in an upstairs room of the house where they were staying (Acts 1:12-14). The twelfth chapter of the same book tells us of a woman named Lydia, who gathered with a group of women outdoors at the river's edge to pray (Acts 16:13). Conversations with God can take place wherever you are because God is everywhere. He's always within earshot.

Often we come before God in prayer with our hands folded. Sometimes we clasp hands in a group. Both are based on tradition, but not specifically mentioned in the Bible. Of course, prayer can be valid, no matter what posture we assume.

Again, I'm reminded of my eldest grandson Cameron, who is now a wonderful young man in his teens. I love his fluency in prayer, no matter where he is. One time he was riding in the car with me, and we were engaged in light conversation. Suddenly, a car zoomed around us on a busy road, swerving somewhat uncontrollably as it went. Cameron said, "that driver must be drinking or something." Immediately he spoke a prayer on behalf of the driver, asking for God to protect him. It came from his lips right where he sat in my car without a second thought. He didn't wait until he could assume a reverent pose or be in a sacred setting. That's how prayer should be—a natural response.

Here are some biblical examples of some possible postures and places for spontaneous prayer:

- Numbers 16:22—Moses and Aaron pleaded to God face down on the ground.
- 1 Kings 8:22-23—King Solomon lifted his hands toward heaven to praise God for who he is and what he does.
- 1 Chronicles 21:16-17—David confessed his sins face down to the ground.
- Psalm 28:2—On another occasion David lifted his hands and cried out for mercy.
- Psalm 95:6—In a hymn of praise David talks about bowing down in worship and kneeling before the Lord.
- Lamentations 2:19—The author (perhaps Jeremiah) talks about rising up during the night to cry out to the Lord with tears flowing and lifting up hands in prayer, pleading on behalf of your children.
- Luke 18:13—A tax collector (a well-known sinner) prayed with his eyes downcast and his body in a humble position, beating his chest in sorrowful repentance.
- Luke 22:41—Jesus, himself, went off to a secluded area, knelt down and had an honest talk with the Father.

Kinds Of Prayer

Do your prayers consist mostly of requests? If so, you are probably not alone. So often we forget the many other things we can and should talk about with God. Here are some other examples of prayer topics:

❖ Daniel 4:34—King Nebuchadnezzar offered a prayer of praise giving God honor and glory for bringing him a feeling of sanity.

❖ 1 John 1:9—John gives us an example of confessing our sins and receiving forgiveness.

❖ 1 Timothy 2:1-2—Paul instructs Timothy, a young pastor, to intercede for all people asking for God's mercy, to give thanks, to pray specifically for leaders and those in authority.

❖ James 5:14-16—James tells us to pray for the sick in faith, believing that God can bring healing. He also says to confess our sins and pray for each other.

❖ Philippians 4:6—Paul and Timothy tell the new believers in Philippi to pray about everything and not worry, to tell God everything they need and thank him for all he has done.

In summary, our lips should be filled with honor and praise as we come to God in prayer. Secondly, it is essential to confess our sins before God, for in confessing we find God faithful to forgive and cleanse us from the blemish of sin. Petitions of all types may be offered including requests for ourselves and for others. We can pray about everything; we need not be bashful about bringing any request to God, big or small. However, we must remember to give thanks in everything, trusting that God knows what is best for us in every circumstance.

Are There Specific Requirements For Prayer?

As we have been observing, there are no "rules" for offering a perfect prayer. However, the Bible does give insight into experiencing effective conversations with God.

We are to pray with confident expectation and in unity with other believers (Matthew 18:19-20). That means Christians come together in prayer with a common goal of letting God be in charge, trusting his answer to be what's best for us. Prayer involves a oneness with God, trusting in him to provide the answer to our greatest problems, needs and concerns. Prayer operates on faith.

God invites intimate, honest, heartfelt prayer—not a showy display of flowery words that don't elicit a listening ear or response from God (Matthew 6). Praying can be more effective, too, if we watchful and alert (Colossians 4:2). That way we will be more likely to hear God's response to us.

We are to pray "in Jesus' name" (John 16:23-24), that is, having a relationship with God through Jesus. It's more than just tacking that phrase onto the end of a prayer. To me, this means trusting Jesus as Savior and Lord and wanting his will to take place in my life. It means not praying answers—I leave the answers up to God and trust they will be the best answer possible.

Ephesians 6:18 tells us to pray at all times on every occasion in the power of the Holy Spirit. This requires submission of our hearts and minds to God so that the Holy Spirit can take over. Pray fervently and never give up.

Why Do My Prayers Seem Unanswered At Times?

Has it ever seemed like God ignored your conversations with him? Could there be some reason for the silence? Or maybe God's response is different than we expect! But then again, the Bible does mention some things that get in the way of our communication with God, and we may need to spend time confessing before requesting.

> "Spend time confessing before requesting."

According to Psalm 66:18-19 confession of our sins is a must if we expect God to listen to our prayers and respond. By the same token we are to forgive those who may have sinned against us if we expect God to forgive us (Matthew 6). There's nothing that can stifle our prayer life or our spiritual growth any quicker than harboring unforgiveness toward someone else—or towards oneself. Unconfessed sin sets up a barricade between our requests and God's answers. It's as if God does not hear the request unless it is funneled through the passageway of confession. Persistence in sins such as following the ways of the wicked, ignoring the needs of the poor and disobeying the laws of God and man have an effect on our ability to receive answers.

Doubt, selfish motives and pride also are factors in receiving appropriate answers to our requests. It is not that God fails to answer the prayer, but rather we fail to receive the answer. James 1:5-8 tells us to ask really expecting an answer. A doubtful mind, says James, is like an "unsettled wave of the sea that is driven and tossed by the wind." He comments further that people in that state should not expect to receive anything from the Lord.

Hearing From God

My husband's vision has been extremely poor ever since he was a small boy. For as long as he can remember, he has worn extremely thick glasses to correct his near-sighted vision. One day when he was in his twenties he felt moved to ask God to be able to see without having to wear glasses. He recalls closing his eyes tightly in submission as he prayed in earnest believing that God was capable of changing his eyesight right then and there. When he opened his eyes he was totally shocked! He was fully expecting to see well without his glasses; however, his vision was exactly as it had been before. Obviously, God did not have the same answer in mind that my husband did.

In the meantime, he received a check for $200 from the state of Indiana where we lived at the time—a bonus acknowledging his service as a Viet Nam veteran. He was discussing how to spend the money with a friend at work. His friend said, "You have been wanting to be able to see without your glasses. Why don't you get contact lenses?" (Contacts were relatively new then.) So, off he went to the eye doctor to pursue this option. Interestingly enough, the exam and contact lenses cost right at $200, so the purchase was made! Was God in that situation? You better believe he was!

God may not answer prayers the way you want or expect; but even if your answer isn't exactly what you perceived, you will receive something from God in the process. Sometimes the unexpected benefits of God's answers far surpass anything we could imagine.

God's words in Jeremiah 33:3 are a profound reminder of what we have at our disposal if we only ask—"Ask me and I will tell you some remarkable secrets about what is going to happen here." Does that not give you encouragement to pray with hopeful expectation?

One of the most important keys to hearing from God is expressed in the words of Jesus in the fifteen chapter of John where he compares our relationship to him as branches being connected to the vine. If we stay joined to him and his words are the nutrition that feeds us, we can ask anything and it will be granted![2]

The Model Prayer

My son, John, and my daughter, Barb, both do a remarkable job teaching their children about prayer. Obviously they have recognized the need for their offspring to know how to communicate with God. Mostly they model it by example. They not only teach their children to pray; they pray *with* them. In my estimation, that is one of the best gifts a parent can give a child. It costs nothing and it's lasting.

> "Prayer . . . the best gift a parent can give a child."

Without a doubt my favorite memories of time spent with my adult children have been in prayer together *(sometimes face down on the floor crying out to God.)* It brings even greater joy as we become aware of God's acknowledgement and take the time to reflect on the unique ways in which he answers.

Apparently, the disciples of Jesus recognized the need for meaningful communication with God, too. They observed Jesus talking to his father in prayer and were curious about the experience. "Lord, teach us to pray" was their request. Jesus responded with what we now commonly call the Lord's Prayer (Matthew 6:9-13). Most of us who grew up with any church affiliation memorized it when we were young children, and many congregations pray this prayer in unison each Sunday.

Certainly, there is power in that prayer when we speak it. But, do you suppose Jesus intended this beautiful example of prayer to be more than just memorized words spoken on a regular basis in church? I believe Jesus was giving his disciples (then and now) a perfect model for prayers—one that contains some very personal elements to conversing with God.

Recently I was having some great one-to-one time with my soon to be 9-years old grandson, Jack. He absolutely loves to hear stories about my childhood experiences since I grew up on the farm. He enjoys hearing about all the farm creatures and my activities back then. It's so different than the lifestyle children in the city experience today. We did discover that some things are similar though. Jack thought it was neat when I told him one of the things I remembered was learning the Lord's Prayer from my dad, since Jack's dad taught him the same prayer. We started talking about what we are actually saying in the prayer and decided to put it in our own words. We came up with something like this:

Our Father which art in heaven, hallowed be thy name.
Heavenly Dad, you're the greatest parent ever! I really respect you.

Thy kingdom come, thy will be done on earth as it is in heaven.
I'll go along with whatever you think is best, Dad…not just for me, but for all my loved ones, too, although I may not always see why you work things out the way you do.

Give us this day our daily bread.
I trust you to supply my food and everything else that I need, not only today, but each day…exactly when I need it.

Forgive us our trespasses as we forgive those who trespass against us.
I've done some wrong things, Dad. Will you please forgive me? And you know those things I've had a hard time forgiving in others?…they're yours God. I don't want to be mad or hateful anymore.

Lead us not into temptation, but deliver us from evil.
I know I'm going to be tempted from time to time, but won't you please lead me in the opposite direction? I know I can't do it on my own.

For thine is the kingdom, and the power, and the glory forever, Amen
Thanks, Dad! You're everything to me. You are just the greatest!

These are all things that should stir in our hearts when we pray the Lord's Prayer. Draw comfort from this prayer as you pray it each Sunday in worship, but also use this prayer as a prominent example in your own personal conversations with God.

Other Examples of Prayer by Jesus

Luke 11:5-13

Jesus continues to teach about prayer by telling a story (parable) about persistence and another about what to expect from a father. God delights in us developing the habit and freedom to ask for help, but he will not leave us trapped in our limited perception of the situation. As "Dad," God knows what is best for us.

John 17

This entire chapter is a powerful prayer offered by Jesus before his arrest. It includes prayer for himself, which reveals the wonderful relationship between Father and Son. It is Jesus' prayer for his disciples and all those who would follow as believers in the future. *(That's us!)*

Back To Your Personal Prayer Life...

Why pray? The answer is very simple. We are to pray because God commands it. God tells us to ask and we will receive. Jesus taught persistence in prayer. We are to ask, and keep on asking. If we are in constant prayer, we will not have the tendency to give up. Prayer serves as an excellent deterrent to temptation. Prayer keeps us from worrying and brings in its place a peace that we are unable to explain or duplicate. Why would we not want to pray with these amazing results a possibility!

Sometimes God answers prayer in dramatic ways. At other times it appears that God hasn't answered at all—at least not yet. Don't despair! If the answers aren't what you expect remember that God knows best. Trust God, and keep on talking while you walk.

You may want to keep a log of some of your conversations with God, just so you can look back and see how God *did* answer them. One of the surprising benefits of praying is how much *we* change in the process. Sometimes that, in itself, is the answer to our prayers.

Chapter Ten

Resting Under The Shadow

Congratulations! You have successfully completed one cycle of your workout and are ready for the "cool down," which is intended to stabilize your heart rate as it brings you into a position of rest. Don't mistake your spiritual cool down with becoming lukewarm in your faith. Rather, it is simply learning to abide in God's presence. It can bring some pretty amazing results if you take the time to do it, and it's where we can be of best service to the Kingdom of God.

Finding The Resting Place

Where is the best place to experience the resting phase of the exercise cycle? My best advice to you is to read Psalm 91. The resting place, according to verse 1, is the "secret place of the Most High" (New King James Version). Another translation calls it a "shelter" denoting a place of protection from harmful elements (New International Version). We are encouraged to dwell or remain for a time in this place of rest. Picture yourself under the protective shadow of the Almighty. That would mean God is very close at hand—surrounding you on all sides, covering you and guarding you. How do you get that close to God? By seeking him with all your heart and soul for the highest good in your life.

Moses comforted the Israelites with this thought in Deuteronomy 4:27-31. Wherever they may have found themselves scattered, they had the security of God's promise to his chosen people. If they would only search after God with every part of their being, they *would* find him. That is an extremely comforting statement to me, for there is as much truth in it for us today as there was for the Israelites. If we seek, we *will* find.

In Matthew 11:28-30 Jesus merely says *come.* "Come to me," he says, "and I will give you rest." Come, you who are weighed down with heavy burdens. Come, you who are bound by the impossible demands of Law. Come, you who are tired of trying to do the right thing only to find you have failed once again. Come.

Jesus' invitation to our tired souls requires but one thing—total surrender on our part. This surrender is made evident by his reference to the yoke (verse 29). You see, there were no motorized vehicles to plow the fields back then. Instead, oxen were used. These oxen were bound together by an oppressive yoke. To a Jew, the yoke stood for harsh submission to authority—precisely what they felt as they labored to keep the Law in an effort to earn their salvation. But Jesus tells us in this passage that *his* yoke is easy. The Greek word here is *chrêstos,* which can mean well-fitting.[1] The yoke Jesus provides is tailor made for each of us and never intended to burden us in any way. In fact, Jesus says his burden is *light.* His invitation to "come" offers salvation by grace rather than through keeping the Law. It is still an act of surrender on our part, but Jesus promises that it won't be oppressive or legalistic. Rather, it is freeing as we gain personal experience in God's grace.

Resting Brings Results!

One of the best things to happen when you abide in Jesus is that you will bear "fruit" (John 15:4-8). That means we will see good results. He tells us that it is impossible to produce good fruit continually unless we abide in him. To abide means to remain, dwell or stay in a place. If you come to a resting place in Jesus, your life will display the evidence, or fruit. Galatians 5:22-23 lists the fruit—love, joy, peace, patience, kindness, goodness, faithfulness, gentleness and self-control. What fantastic characteristics to display! And remember, Jesus said it would be *easy* if you simply come and abide in him!

There is a second result of abiding in God and trusting his perfect plan for you. You can ask God for whatever you desire, and it will be done for you (John 15:7). What a promise that is! You see, if you truly are abiding in Jesus, your desires will be in harmony with his desires. I love the words to the hymn, "Turn Your Eyes Upon Jesus." If our eyes are focused on him, the things of this world become dim in comparison.

A third result of abiding is found in verse 8 of John 15. By abiding in Jesus and bearing good fruit, you will naturally become a disciple—one who accepts the good news of salvation through Jesus and assists in spreading that news to others. That brings glory and honor to God!

Reflecting As You Rest

Every person on earth has the right to walk victoriously in joy and peace, having received full pardon for sins and restoration as a born-again child of the Almighty God. What gives us the right? Throughout this book the message has been clear. Jesus bought that right for us through his death and resurrection. How comforting to know that God's grace is free to everyone who believes. All who labor and are burdened can find rest (Matthew 11:28). Whoever comes to Jesus will not be turned away (John 6:37).

Quite simply put, that's the "good news" you can share! But it's impossible to share something that you don't have or can't identify yourself. Each person has a unique relationship with God. It's your story and only you can tell it; no one else can, because they haven't experienced what

> "It's your story and only you can tell it."

you have. As you abide under the shadow of God, I think it's good to reflect on your personal walk. What are some ways you know for *certain* that God is present in your life. Mediate on these things; offer prayers of thanksgiving as you acknowledge God.

The first thing that comes to mind for me is answered prayer. I have seen God's response to many requests over the years. Secondly, God has changed me from being fearful to "Christ-confident." It's not only apparent to me but to everyone around me. My husband sometimes refers to me as his second wife (although I'm his first and only wife!) because I'm so much different than I was when we first got married. I have a deeply rooted peace that I know comes from God. He calls it the "peace that passes understanding," and I couldn't describe it any better. God continues to give me special gifts and abilities to use for his glory.

Ask yourself these questions: Would it make a difference in my life if I stopped believing in God? If I did not believe Jesus was the Son of God? Is your personal relationship with Jesus important to you? Why? Put your story into words that can be shared with others when the opportunity arises.

Christianity begins with hearing the message of salvation, accepting it, and being welcomed home by God. But the story doesn't end there. What comes next? We are instructed to "pass it on"—to make disciples of anyone and everyone. We are asked to teach people by our words and our actions how to walk in obedience to God.

Jesus told us to *"Go and make disciples of all nations...teaching them to obey everything I have commanded of you"* (Matthew 28:19 NIV).

Don't Stop Here!

Your outreach to others, whether in word or deed, is your response to the faith that God has placed in you. Along with the faith, God gives each one of us the ability to be an effective witness. To be truly effective, we must stay plugged into the power source—the Holy Spirit. Jesus said that when we receive the Spirit, we will automatically respond by witnessing. "When the Holy Spirit has come upon you, you will receive power and will tell people everywhere about me...." (Acts 1:8, *my paraphrase.*) Are you willing to be empowered by God's Spirit? Are you willing to go when God says go and do what God says to do? May God's grace continually rest upon you to be obedient to his voice.

On a final note, remember that exercise is not effective unless it is perpetual. After you have learned to spend time basking in God's presence, start the workout cycle over. Keep searching, studying, pondering and discussing the Word of God. There is wisdom, power, and refreshment in it!

ENDNOTES

Chapter 1

[1]Ronald F. Youngblood, general editor; F.F. Bruce and R.K. Harrison, consulting editors, *Nelson's new illustrated Bible dictionary: Electronic edition of the revised edition of Nelson's illustrated Bible dictionary, Logos Library System*, (Nashville: Thomas Nelson) 1997, c1995.

Chapter 2

[1]Greg Laurie, *The Invisible World: A Look Behind The Scenes of the Supernatural World and Its Effect On Our Lives* (Santa Ana: FBG Distribution 1991), 84.

[2]*Ibid.,* 91.

[3]*Ibid.,* 97.

[4]Greg Laurie, *The Great Compromise,* (Dallas: Word Publishing), 1994.

Chapter 3

[1]*The Quest Study Bible, New International Version,* (Grand Rapids: Zondervan) 1994.

[2]Ronald F. Youngblood, general editor; F.F. Bruce and R.K. Harrison, consulting editors, *Nelson's new illustrated Bible dictionary: Electronic edition of the revised edition of Nelson's illustrated Bible dictionary, Logos Library System*, (Nashville: Thomas Nelson) 1997, c1995.

[3] *The New Word In Life Study Bible, New Testament Edition, New King James Version* (Nashville: Thomas Nelson) 1993.

Chapter 4

[1] W.E.Vine, Merrill F. Unger, William White, Jr; *Vine's Complete Expository Dictionary of Old and New Testament Words*, (Nashville: Thomas Nelson) 1985.

[2] Frank E. Gaebelein, General Editor, *The Expositor's Bible Commentary with The New International Version, Volume 8, pg. 230*, (Grand Rapids: Zondervan) 1984.

[3] *The Living Bible*, (Wheaton: Tyndale) 1971.

Chapter 5

[1] Frank E. Gaebelein, *The Expositor's Bible Commentary with the New International Version, Volume 8*, (Grand Rapids: Zondervan) 1984.

Chapter 6

[1] *The Layman's Bible Encyclopedia*, (Nashville, Tennessee: Southwestern Company), 1964, 310.

[2] Psalm 44:21 (NLT)

[3] *The Oxford Dictionary of Quotations, Third Edition*, (Oxford: Oxford University Press) 1979, 314.

[4] Psalm 51:10

Chapter 7

[1] *The Word In Life Study Bible New Testament Edition*, (Nashville: Thomas Nelson, 1993), 350.

[2] William Barkley, *The Gospel of John, Vol. 1, The Daily Study Bible Series*, Philadelphia: Westminster Press, 1975, 221.

[3] Lift Him Up, Vol. 3 (Benson Company, 1967), 120.

Chapter 8

[1]William Barley, *The Gospel of John, Vol.2, The Daily Bible Series,* (Philadelphia: Westminster Press), 1975, 157.

[2]Ronald F. Youngblood, General editor; Nelson's Illustrated Bible Dictionary, electronic edition, (Nashville: Thomas Nelson Publishers) 1986

[3]Frank E. Gaebelein, General Editor, *The Expositor's Commentary with the New International Version, Vol. 10,* (Grand Rapids: Zondervan) 1984, 246.

[4]*The Quest Study Bible, New International Version,* (Grand Rapids: Zondervan) 1994, 2305.

Chapter 9

[1] Romans 8:26

[2]John 15:7

Chapter 10

[1]William Barclay, *The Daily Study Bible Series, Revised Edition, The Gospel of Matthew, Volume 2,* (Philadelphia:Westminster Press, 1958).